To
Auntie Olwen.

with all my
love.

Andrew.

© **Andrew Owen Reprinted 2015**

7th Edition Reprinted 2015:
ISBN 978-0-9567335-0-4

1st Edition: ISBN 0-9524643-3-0
© Reapers Trust 2001
2nd Edition: ISBN 0-9524643-4-0
© Andrew Owen 2003
3rd Edition: ISBN 0-9524643-6-5
© Andrew Owen 2004
4th Edition: ISBN 0-9524643-7-3
© Andrew Owen 2005
5th Edition: ISBN 0-9524643-8-1
© Andrew Owen 2008
6th Edition: ISBN 0-9567335-0-4
© Andrew Owen 2010

Published in the United Kingdom by
Destiny Leadership Resources:

Destiny
destiny-church.com

Destiny Church
70 Cathedral Street
Glasgow G4 0RN

Tel: 0141 616 6777

All scripture quotations, unless otherwise indicated,
are taken from the New King James Version.
Copyright c 1982 by Thomas Nelson, Inc.
Used by permission. All rights reserved.

Cover Design: Grafica, Glasgow
Typesetting: Verve GRP, Glasgow
Printed by Bell and Bain Ltd, Glasgow

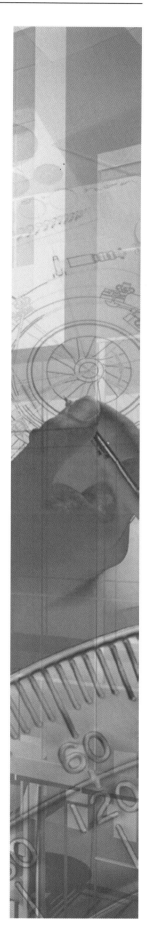

Welcome!

Welcome to this study. I am excited about the future and passionate about the church. A whole new generation of people are rising up – people like you – who want to live with a real faith in a real world.

At one time Moses was warned by God, when he was about to build the tabernacle:

> **'See that you make all things ACCORDING TO THE PATTERN shown you on the mountain.'**
> Hebrews 8:5

The tabernacle was a portable tent-like structure that played a very significant role in the history of Israel. Moses, who was commissioned in its building, was instructed by God to pay attention to what he built because, due to its importance, it had to be exact. Therefore the title is appropriate for our study, in that God is still in the building business. He builds lives, He is building His church, and all because He still loves this world passionately. Thankfully He has given us a fantastic blueprint, a book of specific instructions – THE BIBLE. It's practical, faith-producing and if we will live by it, we will make our world different.

This study is not about your opinion or mine, but a closer look at what the Bible actually says on a number of important issues. I'm sure that as you study, you will find the scriptures to be challenging, exciting and life giving.

May you be blessed, as you build your life 'according to the pattern'.

Andrew Owen

© Andrew Owen Reprinted 2015 email: dlr@destiny-church.com
Destiny Church, 70 Cathedral Street, Glasgow, G4 0RN
Follow us on Twitter @andrewdestiny @OwenSue @DLR3000   Visit our website www.destinyleadershipresources.com

My Personal Notes

Pre-Course Reading

Getting to grips with the Bible

© Andrew Owen Reprinted 2015 email: dlr@destiny-church.com
Destiny Church, 70 Cathedral Street, Glasgow, G4 0RN
Follow us on Twitter @andrewdestiny @OwenSue @DLR3000   Visit our website www.destinyleadershipresources.com

My Personal Notes

The following information will help you understand the Bible and get the most out of this course:

Why Study The Bible?

We believe it to be God's word.

> *'All scripture is given by inspiration of God, and is profitable for doctrine, for reproof, for correction, for instruction in righteousness,'*
> 2 Timothy 3:16

We believe it to be God's way.

> *'Your word is a lamp to my feet and a light to my path.'*
> Psalm 119:105

We know it produces faith.

> *'So then faith comes by hearing, and hearing by the word of God.'*
> Romans 10:17

It causes both our personal and corporate success.

> *'This Book of the Law shall not depart from your mouth, but you shall meditate in it day and night, that you may observe to do according to all that is written in it. For then you will make your way prosperous, and then you will have good success.'*
> Joshua 1:8

It brings healing.

> *'He sent His word and healed them, and delivered them from their destructions.'*
> Psalm 107:20

It contains the nutrition required for a full life.

> *'But He answered and said, "It is written, 'Man shall not live by bread alone, but by every word that proceeds from the mouth of God'*
> Matthew 4:4

It challenges us and takes us to a higher level.

> *'For the word of God is living and powerful, and sharper than any two-edged sword, piercing even to the division of soul and spirit, and of joints and marrow, and is a discerner of the thoughts and intents of the heart.'*
> Hebrews 4:12

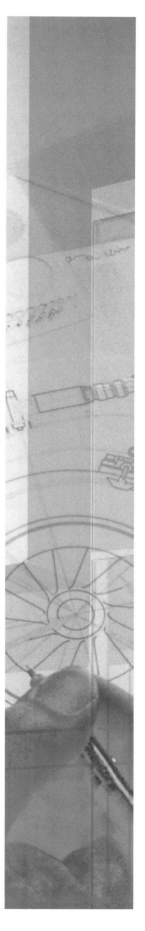

We discover God Himself this way.

> *'With my whole heart I have sought You; Oh, let me not wander from Your commandments!'*
> Psalm 119:10

How Did We Get The Bible?

Although God is the author of the Bible, He used people to write it. He used many different authors, including kings, farmers, doctors, fishermen, shepherds and priests. You can often see their personalities in the way they wrote, but God watched over the whole process – that is why the Bible fits together so perfectly.

> *'...knowing this first, that no prophecy of Scripture is of any private interpretation, for prophecy never came by the will of man, but holy men of God spoke as they were moved by the Holy Spirit.'*
> 2 Peter 1:20-21

These books were collected together, guarded and copied down through the years. They were included in the 'canon' of scripture (collection of inspired writings). All 66 books (39 in the Old Testament and 27 in the New Testament) have met certain tests, which set them apart from other religious writings. (Did you know that the word 'Bible' comes from the Latin and means 'library'?)

At the time of Jesus, the 'Bible' consisted of what we know as the Old Testament. In Jesus' day a Greek translation of the Old Testament was used, known as the 'Septuagint'. Jesus himself recognised these books as being God's word; He quoted the Old Testament and reprimanded people for ignoring it, for example:

> *'...Thus you have made the commandment of God of no effect by your tradition.'*
> Matthew 15:6

After Jesus' time on earth other books were added to this collection. They were written by eye-witnesses of Jesus' life and recognised church leaders, and quickly received recognition as having God's authority; for example, Paul's letters were called 'scripture'. (2 Peter 3:16)

Since the Bible was completed, it has been translated into hundreds of languages and distributed widely. It remains the world's best selling book, so consistently at No 1 in the best sellers lists that it is no longer listed!

© Andrew Owen Reprinted 2015 email: dlr@destiny-church.com
Destiny Church, 70 Cathedral Street, Glasgow, G4 0RN
Follow us on Twitter @andrewdestiny @OwenSue @DLR3000   Visit our website www.destinyleadershipresources.com

You will notice straight away that the Bible is split into two unequal sections. The largest covers the period up to the time of Jesus, and is called 'the Old Testament'. It falls into a further five sections. Get out your Bible and check the following list against your 'contents' page.

Books are not placed in historical or date order. (The last historical point in the Old Testament is Nehemiah - 400 BC).

OLD TESTAMENT:

Law or Pentateuch	*Genesis* *Exodus* *Leviticus* *Numbers* *Deuteronomy*

The Law:

The first 5 books cover the early history of mankind, and especially that of the Israelites. Mostly written by Moses, one of the main themes is the commandments that God gave to His people, including the well - known ten commandments'. (Exodus 20)

History	*Joshua* *Judges* *Ruth* *1 Samuel* *2 Samuel* *1 Kings* *2 Kings* *1 Chronicles* *2 Chronicles* *Ezra* *Nehemiah* *Esther*

History:

From Joshua to Esther we find the story of the people of Israel, including all their great successes when they followed God, as well as their failures when they rejected Him. There are many important lessons for us to learn here.

Wisdom And Poetry Books:

Wisdom or Poetry	*Job* *Psalms* *Proverbs* *Ecclesiastes* *Song of Solomon*

From Job to the Song of Solomon, you will find every emotion and experience you will ever encounter. You will discover how to pray, how to express yourself in praise and worship, and where to find wisdom for every one of life's challenges.

© Andrew Owen Reprinted 2015 email: dlr@destiny-church.com
Destiny Church, 70 Cathedral Street, Glasgow, G4 0RN
Follow us on Twitter @andrewdestiny @OwenSue @DLR3000   Visit our website www.destinyleadershipresources.com

Major Prophets	Isaiah Jeremiah Lamentations Ezekiel Daniel
Minor Prophets	Hosea Joel Amos Obadiah Jonah Micah Nahum Habakkuk Zephaniah Haggai Zechariah Malachi

The Prophets:

Isaiah to Malachi are the prophetic books, which are not so much concerned with telling the future as with expressing exactly how God feels and thinks about all that happens here on earth.

'Now all these things happened to them as examples, and they were written for our admonition,'
1 Corinthians 10:11

NEW TESTAMENT:

4 Gospels:	
Synoptic Gospels:	Matthew Mark Luke
Gospel:	John
History:	Acts

The Gospels:

The first four books deal specifically with the life, death and resurrection of Jesus, covering the same ground from four different perspectives. They are accurate in detail (Luke 1:1-4) but were not just written to record history.

'but these are written that you may believe that Jesus is the Christ, the Son of God, and that believing you may have life in His Name.'
John 20:31

Acts:

Contains the history of the early church and its spread across Europe and Asia. It gives us a good idea of what our church life should be like and keys to its growth.

© Andrew Owen Reprinted 2015 email: dlr@destiny-church.com
Destiny Church, 70 Cathedral Street, Glasgow, G4 0RN
Follow us on Twitter @andrewdestiny @OwenSue @DLR3000   Visit our website www.destinyleadershipresources.com

Letters or Epistles:	Romans 1 Corinthians 2 Corinthians Galatians Ephesians Philippians Colossians 1 Thessalonians 2 Thessalonians 1 Timothy 2 Timothy Titus Philemon Hebrews James 1 Peter 2 Peter 1 John 2 John 3 John Jude

The Epistles:

These are letters to churches and to individuals in them. They contain large sections of teaching with much advice on how to put it into practice, and sometimes deal with specific problems that had arisen in the different churches.

Prophecy:	Revelation

Revelation: is the only book of prophecy in the New Testament. Seemingly difficult to understand at first, its unusual symbolic language contains a message of great encouragement.

The Bible Has One Central Character - Jesus Christ

The Old Testament constantly looks forward to Jesus, and the New Testament always refers back to Him. He is the centre of all that the Bible says, and if you keep Him at the centre of your life, the Bible will open its secrets to you.

> **'You search the Scriptures, for in them you think you have eternal life; and these are they which testify of Me.'**
> John 5:39

The Bible is like -

A Plumb Line

Every builder needs a plumb line, or else even the simplest wall could be built out of line. The Bible provides a standard against which we

can measure every part of our lives to ensure that they are being built straight and true.

A Sword (Hebrews 4:12)

It will often challenge us to cut some things out and leave some things behind.

A Healing Oil (Psalm 107:20)

When we have been hurt, the word of God often produces healing within us.

What Should I Do?

Read: Some of the smaller books you could read in one go, and you might also like to have a plan – perhaps to read the whole Bible through in one year. Read at least some of the Bible every day and ask God to speak to you. Expect Him to help you understand the passages you look at.

> *'Man shall not live by bread alone, but by every word that proceeds from the mouth of God.'*
> Matthew 4:4

Don't struggle with difficult sections, but get to know the simpler parts first – that will make the rest of the Bible easier to understand. If you have not read much of the Bible before, start with one of the gospels, and the Psalms.

Study: Sometimes you can take one passage of a book and investigate it in depth. Bible characters and themes also make good subjects. Here are some rules to help you study.

Always try to find out what the author originally meant – put yourself in his shoes.

Interpret difficult parts of the Bible by looking at easier parts for help. The best interpreter of the Bible is the Bible. This gets easier the more you know of the Bible.

Memorise: God will speak to you from the Bible, and it is good to develop the habit of memorising particular verses that He uses to say something to you. The verses you learn can be invaluable to you later on. Jesus, for example, quoted from the Bible in order to overcome temptation. (Matthew 4:4,7,10)

© Andrew Owen Reprinted 2015 email: dlr@destiny-church.com
Destiny Church, 70 Cathedral Street, Glasgow, G4 0RN
Follow us on Twitter @andrewdestiny @OwenSue @DLR3000   Visit our website www.destinyleadershipresources.com

Meditate: This does not mean to empty your mind, but rather to fill it with thoughts from the Bible:

> *'But his delight is in the law of the Lord, and in His law he meditates day and night. He shall be like a tree planted by the rivers of water, that brings forth its fruit in its season, whose leaf also shall not wither; and whatever he does shall prosper.'*
> Psalm 1:2-3

Meditation usually means taking just a few verses rather than a whole book, and 'chewing' them over in your mind and heart.

Obey: As we said at the beginning, this book is given for a purpose – to bring direction and meaning to our lives, and to help us fulfil the plan that God has for us. The Bible will be interesting to read - but the greatest blessing comes when we <u>DO IT</u>!

> *'But he who looks into the perfect law of liberty and continues in it, and is not a forgetful hearer but a doer of the work, this one will be blessed in what he does.'*
> James 1:25

Statement

We believe the Bible to be God's word. It is both infallible and timeless, and is our final authority on all matters. It takes priority over experience or tradition in our lives. It will produce faith within us, and with that faith we can overcome every challenge.

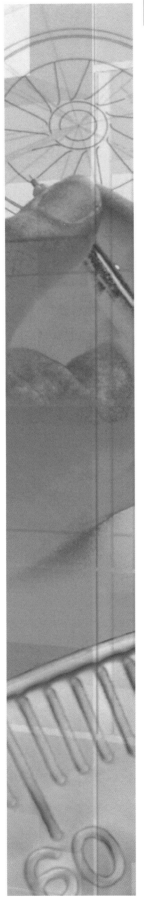

My Personal Notes

According to the Pattern

essential truth for an exceptional life

Study 1

Real Faith

My Personal Notes

Jesus of Nazareth

Today in our world, Christianity so often means no more than another religion to be set along side other faiths like Islam, Hinduism or Buddhism for example. In fact "Christian" was not a term the early believers used of themselves, but a nickname given to them. (Acts 11: 26) They considered themselves to be followers of Jesus of Nazareth. Therefore the question of real faith does not revolve around the religion you have, but around the person of Jesus of Nazareth. As we have so often seen, all religion divides, but when we look at the teachings and claims of Jesus, we find something altogether different. Jesus never claimed to come to start a religion, but He did claim that He came to give us life.

"In Him (Jesus) was life, and that life was the light of men" John 1:4

Let's take a few moments to consider God's view of man's situation, and the teachings and claims of Jesus of Nazareth in the light of this.

What Does God Say About Men And Women?

Most people at some time try to find an answer to the question 'why am I here?' There are two great days in the life of an individual: the day they were born, and the day they knew why they were born. The Bible provides the only correct solution to the puzzle. God created man in His own image and likeness (Genesis 1:26-31) and gave him the opportunity to have a full, successful and eternal life, to be enjoyed with God Himself. God did not make man as a computer – to obey Him automatically, but gave man a will to love and freedom to choose. Sadly, man chose to disobey God (Genesis 3:1-19), and to go his own rebellious way. From that moment on, Adam brought sin into the world (Romans 5:19) - and there's no point blaming Adam, because all of us have made the same choice!

What Is The Position Now?

The position is very clear. God highlighted the standards we must reach if we are to be restored into His family. As we are all now sinners, first by birth and then by practice, we miss the mark and we can never, in our own right, attain to the standard or make the grade.

When God gave the law (ten commandments), He was not just saying 'here is a standard – reach it', but also providing a measuring tape – to show us by how much we miss it! We need help! No-one can reach it!

'There is none righteous, no, not one;'
Romans 3:10

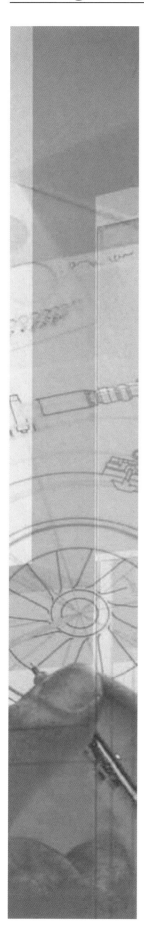

Sin

Sin is totally repulsive to God, and the most destructive force on this planet. It is sin that causes death. Sin is so powerful that the Bible calls it 'the law of sin and death (Romans 8:2). Just as gravity pulls you down, so does sin. It will eventually destroy you completely if not dealt with.

> *'Then, when desire has conceived, it gives birth to sin; and sin, when it is full-grown, brings forth death.'*
> James 1:15

Sin means: 'to miss the mark'
              'a governing force or power'
              'a sinful act or deed'
              'acts of disobedience to divine law'
              'a crossing over the line'

This is now the situation – there is a great gulf between man and God, because of sin.

This gulf between man and God is the greatest human tragedy ever! It has left people empty and, contrary to evolutionary theories, only a caricature of what they were intended to be. The only answer to life's question 'why am I here and what is it all about?' is to come home to the God who made you – only He can fill the inner longings of your heart. But how?

How Can This Gulf Be Bridged?

Not by:-

◈   Working for it (Ephesians 2:8-9)

◈   Being naturally born into it (John 1:13)

◈   Being religious (Galatians 3:2-3)

◈   Following any alternative religion - (John 14:6)
     they don't all lead to God

But by:-

Being '**BORN AGAIN**'. To have such an experience is the most important thing in the world for you as an individual. You have to have a new beginning – a fresh start!

© Andrew Owen Reprinted 2015 email: dlr@destiny-church.com
Destiny Church, 70 Cathedral Street, Glasgow, G4 0RN
Follow us on Twitter @andrewdestiny @OwenSue @DLR3000   Visit our website www.destinyleadershipresources.com

'... Do not marvel that I said to you, 'You must be born again.'
John 3:6-7

Jesus taught something very different to all religions. Religion is built and based on rules and regulations where man tries to reach up to God. But Jesus taught that in fact God reached down to man. He made it quite clear, that man cannot save himself. He needs a saviour. Receiving this life from God, which Jesus described as being "born again", requires some very simple, but very important steps.

The first it to realise that you and I **personally** need a saviour, and that God has provided only one- JESUS!

'Nor is there salvation in any other, for there is no other name under heaven given among men by which we must be saved.'
Acts 4:12

Why Is Jesus The ONLY Answer?

1.   He made that claim himself (John 14:6).

2.   God the Father endorsed that claim (Acts 17:31).

3.   Jesus had no sin (2 Corinthians 5:21). All men sin and will die for their sins. We cannot save ourselves because we are all guilty.

    'for all have sinned and fall short of the glory of God'
    Romans 3:23

4.   He is the only one able to give to us the gift of "righteousness" (1 Corinthians 1:30)

5.   He wants to save us (Acts 2:21).

6.   He is alive to save us (Romans 5:10).

Question! What do you think of Jesus' claims?

How Do I Get Saved?

God has made it so easy for us.
    '... if you confess with your mouth the Lord Jesus and believe in your heart that God has raised Him from the dead, you will be saved. For with the heart one believes unto righteousness, and with the mouth confession is made unto salvation.'
    Romans 10:9-10

The Greek word for 'saved' is 'sozo', which means to make whole again, to deliver, to heal rescue and protect.

You get saved by:

1.   Seeing your need (2 Corinthians 7:10)

2.   Turning around. The Bible calls this 'repentance'.

We must repent from <u>two</u> things:

i)   <u>Sin</u>: the Bible talks of sin as being not only wrong ACTIONS   but also wrong ATTITUDES. It gives examples of sin, such as:

> *'Now the works of the flesh are evident,*
> *which are: adultery, fornication, uncleanness,*
> *lewdness, idolatry, sorcery, hatred,*
> *contentions, jealousies, outbursts of wrath,*
> *selfish ambitions, dissensions, heresies,*
> *envy, murders, drunkenness, revelries, and*
> *the like;*
> Galatians 5:19-21

We must turn our backs on these things.

ii)   <u>Dead Works</u>:

> *'...not laying again the foundation of*
> *repentance from dead works and of faith*
> *toward God.'*
> Hebrews 6:1

This includes activities that we undertake in an effort to try and WORK our way out of sin. They often include charitable deeds or religious activities that are in our thinking; ways of scoring points with God. Church or temple attendance, or prayers to saints or other gods won't work. We need to remember nothing we can naturally do will change the situation. We need a Saviour.

3.   Faith In Jesus

> *'...repentance toward God and faith toward*
> *our Lord Jesus Christ.'*
> Acts 20:21

Commonly faith is seen as 'having a faith', that is, having a set of beliefs or a particular religion that you follow. God's idea of faith is far more than that. To have faith in someone means that you totally believe and therefore live acting on what that person has done or said. The Bible teaches us that it is God's desire that all men should find him.

> **'But without faith it is impossible to please Him, for he who comes to God must believe that He is, and that He is a rewarder of those who diligently seek Him.'**
> Hebrews 11:6

Some people say that they are 'atheists' – they do not believe in the existence of God. Others would say they are 'agnostics' – that is, they do not know if God exists. But real faith brings us into fellowship with God.

> **'Now faith is the substance of things hoped for, the evidence of things not seen.'**
> Hebrews 11:1

We should also note that the Bible tells us – God has given faith to <u>everyone</u> (Romans 12:3). It is like this – God gave me the gift of 'sight'; when I am seeing, that is me using the gift. God has given to all the gift of 'faith'; when I am believing, that is me using that gift!
Having faith in God therefore means to place your whole life into the hands of Jesus.

> **"This is the work of God to believe in the one whom he has sent"** John 6:29

A present is no good to anyone if it is left in the box; it actually becomes yours when you reach out and take it by faith.

4. Make It Yours By:
a)   Asking God to forgive you and save you (Acts 2:21).
b)   Believe that He will and so make you righteous and fully acceptable before the father (Matthew 21:22)
c)   Tell others that you have become a follower and believer in Jesus (Romans 10:9)

> **'...that if you confess with your mouth ...'**
> Romans 10:9

5. Begin This New Life With Good Habits

Just as a baby needs food and a family to grow, so do we.
i)   Read and pray regularly (1 Peter 2:2)
ii)   Live right and set out to please God (1 John 2:29)
iii)   Be committed to and an active part of the local church (Psalm 92:13).
iv)   Don't give up. Ask God to help you (John 16:33; 1 John 5:4).

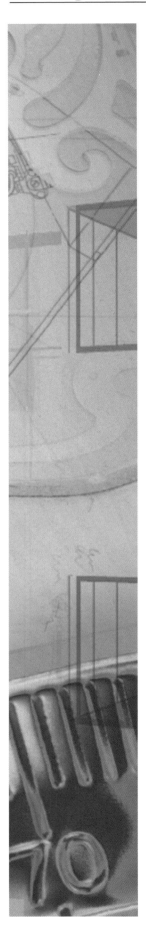

Moving On

> '*And Jesus came and spoke to them, saying, "All authority has been given to Me in heaven and on earth. "Go therefore and make disciples of all the nations, baptizing them in the name of the Father and of the Son and of the Holy Spirit,'*
> Matthew 28:18-19

God seldom goes in for ceremonies in the church. The life He gives is a matter for the heart. But here is one ceremony that He commands. As we look at the scriptures we will see that water baptism is very closely linked with salvation. It is more than a ceremony, in that it actually does something in you when appropriated by faith.

What Is Baptism?

For many, the term baptism represents infants being sprinkled over a font, a tradition of some churches. This, however, has no validity anywhere in scripture. The only baptism the Bible teaches is BELIEVERS' baptism by immersion. Repentance must be in operation first.

> '*...Repent, and let every one of you be baptised in the name of Jesus Christ for the remission of sins; and you shall receive the gift of the Holy Spirit.'*
> Acts 2:38

The case for this is as follows:

1. The Meaning Of The Word

The original Greek term for baptism is 'baptizo'. This term was frequently used by the Greeks for dyeing a garment. The cloth was said to be baptised when it was completely coloured. Occasionally it was used of a ship that had sunk and become a wreck, or of drawing water by immersing one vessel in another. Its strongest meaning is to 'submerge' or 'plunge'.

2. The Biblical Examples Given

Some examples of water baptism:

- ❖   Philip in Samaria (Acts 8:9-12)
- ❖   Philip and the Ethiopian (Acts 8:26-40)
- ❖   Paul, Silas and the jailor (Acts 16: 30-34)

© Andrew Owen Reprinted 2015 email: dlr@destiny-church.com
Destiny Church, 70 Cathedral Street, Glasgow, G4 0RN
Follow us on Twitter @andrewdestiny @OwenSue @DLR3000   Visit our website www.destinyleadershipresources.com

3. <u>Why Must I Be Baptised?</u>

When you are baptised as a believer in Christ, you are following Jesus in several experiences of His life. (Read Romans 6:1-4)

i)   His death
ii)   His burial
iii)   His resurrection

You must get baptised because:

a)   Jesus commands it. Followers follow their leader!
b)   You need to die to old habits, sins and God-offending lifestyles.
c)   We bury bodies because they stink!

> *'Brethren, I do not count myself to have apprehended; but one thing I do, forgetting those things which are behind and reaching forward to those things which are ahead'*
> Philippians 3:13

d)   To live a new dedicated life (Galatians 2:20)

Build On The Foundation

> *'of the doctrine of baptisms, of laying on of hands, of resurrection of the dead, and of eternal judgment.'*
> Hebrews 6:2

A foundation is something you can build on. You are meant to build on this experience by:

1.   Not living with guilt and condemnation

> *'There is therefore now no condemnation to those who are in Christ Jesus, who do not walk according to the flesh, but according to the Spirit'*
> Romans 8:1

2.   Using the experience to overcome temptation

> *'Likewise you also, reckon yourselves to be dead indeed to sin, but alive to God in Christ Jesus our Lord. Therefore do not let sin reign in your mortal body, that you should obey it in its lusts. And do not present your members as instruments of unrighteousness to sin, but present yourselves to God as being alive from the dead, and your members as instruments of righteousness to God.'*
> Romans 6:11-13

When Should I Get Baptised?

As soon as possible! (Acts 8:12)
Baptism should not be delayed. It's a step <u>towards</u> maturity - not a reward for it!

Stop! Before Moving On!

Check List

The Bible on more than one occasion gives us examples of people who had to deal with past experiences and current practices before they could move on with God. In Acts we read of how they burned all their occult books in the streets. Do you have something that needs to be dealt with at this point? Here's a checklist (which may not be exhaustive), go through them allowing the Holy Spirit to direct you. Most probably you'll deal with them on your own – but if you feel the need to talk to someone don't hesitate to call your local pastor for help. Don't be afraid to face them, and call on God's help to leave them behind you.

Past / present involvements that may need cutting off or a change of lifestyle: these things can negatively affect your life.

Sexual immorality: - this includes living together outside of marriage or sex outside of marriage, even with a consenting partner - pornography - homosexuality	Addictions Dishonesty Fears and phobias Religious entanglements Occult/spiritualistic practices Violence and anger

If you possess books, tapes or videos that promote these issues, you should dispose of them. Don't allow them to influence your life any longer. If you are in a wrong kind of relationship, put it right as soon as you are able.

Some attitudes of heart that hinder: these heart issues can have the greatest negative effect.

Bitterness Hatred Envy Unforgiveness	Jealousy Pride Covetousness

You <u>must</u> deal with your heart – or it will deal with you.

If any of the above lists are relevant to you, God is both a wonderful healer and deliverer. Look to Him to set you free. Consider seeing a Christian counsellor, such as your pastor, if you need further help.

You should spend some time praying, seeking God's forgiveness and forgiving others who have hurt you before you move on. .

© Andrew Owen Reprinted 2015 email: dlr@destiny-church.com
Destiny Church, 70 Cathedral Street, Glasgow, G4 0RN
Follow us on Twitter @andrewdestiny @OwenSue @DLR3000   Visit our website www.destinyleadershipresources.com

According to the Pattern

essential truth for an exceptional life

Study 2

Empowered

The Gospel of God

The gospel (good news) is called the gospel of GOD in Romans 1:1. The Bible reveals God to be a triune God. God the Father, God the Son, and God the Holy Spirit.

The gospel-this amazing message was the Father's idea. We read "God so loved the world that he sent his only Son..." (John 3:16). The Bible also tells us GOD IS LOVE (1 John 4:16). We have already seen that sin separates us from God the Father. BUT the Father -because of this great love sent the SON to save us. And Jesus Christ-God's son came to both die for our sins and gift us with this all important factor "righteousness". We have this gift which empowers us to have such a wonderful position before God the Father. Jesus came to bring us back to the Father, and know and experience his love and grace.

"And this is life eternal, that they might know thee-the only true God, and Jesus Christ, who thou hast sent" (KJV. John 17:3).

Some people only think of God the Father as someone very austere-but just look how much he loves, and the lengths he went to bring us into this relationship with himself. Look how much Jesus loves you-in that he was willing to do all of this. Maybe-you have had a very negative experience of a father? Then let your ideas, thoughts and experiences be changed, as you come and experience a real fathers love in God.

Now-further, since we are so acceptable before God-he sends his Holy Spirit, to live in our hearts, and totally empower and transform our lives. We now look at the work and person of the Holy Spirit. And see and understand that this is the gospel of GOD, Father, Son and Spirit are fully involved .

© Andrew Owen Reprinted 2015 email: dlr@destiny-church.com
Destiny Church, 70 Cathedral Street, Glasgow, G4 0RN
Follow us on Twitter @andrewdestiny @OwenSue @DLR3000   Visit our website www.destinyleadershipresources.com

Empowered

If you were leaving your closest friends to go on a very long journey, and you had the opportunity to say a last few words, what would you say? One thing is certain, it would be important.

Jesus, in His last conversation on earth with the disciples, emphasised the need to have this experience with the Holy Spirit:

> *'And being assembled together with them, He commanded them not to depart from Jerusalem, but to wait for the Promise of the Father, "which"' He said "you have heard from Me;"'*
> Acts 1:4

> *But you shall receive power when the Holy Spirit has come upon you;'*
> Acts 1:8

Who is the Holy Spirit?

> *'I did not know Him, but He who sent me to baptize with water said to me, "Upon whom you see the Spirit descending, and remaining on Him, this is He who baptizes with the Holy Spirit."'*
> John 1:33

We believe in the 'Trinity'; that there is ONE God, who exists in three persons: Father, Son and Holy Spirit.

The Holy Spirit is mentioned more than ninety times in the Old Testament, and more than two hundred and sixty times in the New Testament, together with more than 39 different names or titles. In the Old Testament the Holy Spirit was only poured out on a few people; the hope then, which is now fulfilled, was that the Holy Spirit would be poured out on <u>all</u> of God's people. (Acts 2:39)

The Holy Spirit is:

i)   A person, not an 'influence'. (John 14:16-17; 1 John 5:6)

ii)   Divine. (Acts 5:3-4; 1 Corinthians 3:16)
       Omnipotent – 'all powerful'. (Luke 1:35)
       Omniscient – 'all knowing'. (John 14:26)
       Omnipresent – 'everywhere'. (Psalm 139:7-10)

iii)   Described as the 'breath' of God. This implies that He is the
       unseen force at work in our lives and in the world (John 3:5-8).

Anointing!

To Old Testament readers, the concept of 'anointing' was both a privilege and a necessity. The word 'anointing' means 'to rub on'. The person set apart for an important and particular task had to be 'anointed' – usually with oil.

For example:　　　　David as king (1 Samuel 16:13)
　　　　　　　　　　Aaron as priest (Leviticus 4:5)

Anointing signified:　God's approval of the man
　　　　　　　　　　God's appointing to the office
　　　　　　　　　　God's authority to accomplish the task
　　　　　　　　　　God's association to the purpose
　　　　　　　　　　God's account to meet the need

To touch or withstand an anointed person was seen as withstanding God himself. Hence David would not touch King Saul, even though Saul sought his life, since Saul was 'the Lord's anointed' (1 Samuel 26:16).

Jesus is the 'Christ', which means 'Messiah', or 'Anointed One' (Luke 4:18). God wants the same anointing on us.

> *'If you then, being evil, know how to give good gifts to your children, how much more will your heavenly Father give the Holy Spirit to those who ask Him!'*
> Luke 11:13

Introducing the Baptism in the Holy Spirit

'Baptism in the Holy Spirit' is a biblical term.

> *'... but He who is coming after me is mightier than I, whose sandals I am not worthy to carry. He will baptize you with the Holy Spirit and fire.'*
> Matthew 3:11

(Also see: Mark 1:8; Luke 3:16; John 1:33; Acts 1:5; Acts 11:16; 1 Corinthians 12:13)

Someone has said, when you get baptised in water you have God, but when you get baptised in the Holy Spirit God has you.
You will remember that 'to baptise' means 'to totally immerse'! It is an act of total trust and abandonment in an encounter with God. While

© Andrew Owen Reprinted 2015 email: dlr@destiny-church.com
Destiny Church, 70 Cathedral Street, Glasgow, G4 0RN
Follow us on Twitter @andrewdestiny @OwenSue @DLR3000　Visit our website www.destinyleadershipresources.com

this begins as an initial experience, the Bible encourages us then to be continually filled with the Holy Spirit (Ephesians 5:18).

Who is This Baptism For?

The baptism in the Holy Spirit is intended for ALL believers.

> *'For the promise is to you and to your children, and to all who are afar off, as many as the Lord our God will call.'*
> Acts 2:39

According to scripture this experience is considered as a necessary foundation for every believer, and not an optional extra.

> *'Therefore, leaving the discussion of the elementary principles of Christ, let us go on to perfection, not laying again the foundation of repentance from dead works and of faith toward God, of the doctrine of baptisms,'*
> Hebrews 6:1-2

Acts 9:18/19 Acts 19:6

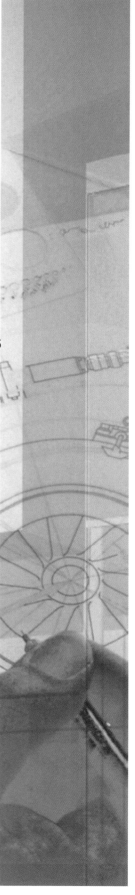

How Do You Receive This Gift?

We have five instances in the book of Acts of people receiving this gift (Acts 2; Acts 8: Acts 9:18/19 Acts 10: Acts 19:6). They either received it as a sovereign act of God or by the laying on of the hands of those already baptised.

The two occasions of divine intervention (Acts 2; Acts 10) do appear to be exceptions. In one case, it was the first giving of the Holy Spirit, and in the other Peter's prejudices would never have allowed him to lay hands on Gentiles. The norm, it would appear, is through the laying on of hands. This is when others who have already received the Holy Spirit put their hands on you, and pray over you. You should also note that out of these five examples, four show that the people were already believers – indicating this experience is often separate to the initial steps of conversion.

Your part is first to have:

◈   Repented from your sin   (Acts 2:38)
◈   Asked for this gift   (Luke 11:13)

God's part is:

◈   You'll receive it from him (Acts 2:39)

As with all aspects of the believer's life, you receive it by faith (James 4:8).

What Should I Expect?

1. To be filled to overflowing.

    'He who believes in Me, as the Scripture has said, out of his heart will flow rivers of living water. But this He spoke concerning the Spirit, whom those believing in Him would receive;'
    John 7:38-39

2. To speak in tongues.

    One clear evidence of this infilling and overflow is a supernatural gift enabling you to speak with other tongues.

    'And they were all filled with the Holy Spirit and began to speak with other tongues, as the Spirit gave them utterance.'
    Acts 2:4

    This language consists of words and syllables that you won't have learned in school. Instead, it is a language that the Holy Spirit gives to enable you to speak and pray without the hindrances of natural thought. It comes from within your spirit, not your mind. This new ability is for <u>every</u> person who is baptized in the Holy Spirit.

3. Prophecy.

    In one place (Ephesus) people who received the baptism in the Holy Spirit also prophesied! (Acts 19)

    'And it shall come to pass in the last days, says God, That I will pour out of My Spirit on all flesh; Your sons and your daughters shall prophesy,'
    Acts 2:17

    'I wish you all spoke with tongues, but even more that you prophesied;'
    1 Corinthians 14:5

© Andrew Owen Reprinted 2015 email: dlr@destiny-church.com
Destiny Church, 70 Cathedral Street, Glasgow, G4 0RN
Follow us on Twitter @andrewdestiny @OwenSue @DLR3000   Visit our website www.destinyleadershipresources.com

4.   Power to witness. (Acts 1:8)

An injunction given to each one of us is to witness to the life of Jesus (Mark 16:15; Matthew 28:19). Frequently fear and a sense of inadequacy stop us. The Holy Spirit becomes the power within us - we speak up, tell them about Jesus and / or invite them to church.

5.   Power in prayer.

He gives us a new language known as 'tongues', to be used in prayer and praise. It is important to use this language as it is useful in making us strong (1 Corinthians 14:4; Romans 8:26-27). Paul claimed he spoke in tongues more than anybody.

6.   **The gifts of the Spirit become available to you.**

In 1 Corinthians 12:8-10 you will observe that there are nine gifts, and that they fall into three categories as follows:

Inspiration: Word of wisdom
                   Word of knowledge
                   Discerning of spirits

Demonstration: Gifts of healings
                   Working of miracles
                   Faith

Communication: Prophecy
                   Different kinds of tongues
                   Interpretation of tongues

The word for gifts is 'charisma', which means a gift of grace – it is not something that is earned.

The early apostles were called to be witnesses of the resurrection. The manifestation of these supernatural gifts confirms the power of the risen Christ.

'The gift' that you receive is the 'Holy Spirit'! Since He has all the gifts – on receiving Him you receive them all – with the possibility and potential of operating in each!

© Andrew Owen Reprinted 2015 email: dlr@destiny-church.com
Destiny Church, 70 Cathedral Street, Glasgow, G4 0RN
Follow us on Twitter @andrewdestiny @OwenSue @DLR3000   Visit our website www.destinyleadershipresources.com

7.   To be enabled to win the battle over sin.

     'For if you live according to the flesh you will die; but if by the Spirit you put to death the deeds of the body, you will live.'
     Romans 8:13

8.   To be changed to become like Jesus, and to conquer your private world.

     By:

     ❖   Giving me power over sin (Romans 8:13)
     ❖   Confirming to me that I am part of God's family
         (Romans 8:16)
     ❖   Helping me to pray properly (Romans 8:26)
     ❖   Helping me to renew my mind and change my thinking
         (2 Timothy 1:7)

9.   To change the world!

     The Holy Spirit is:

     a)   Convicting people of their need of Jesus (John 16:8)
     b)   Empowering me to make change (1 John 5:4)

          - In my life
          - In my home
          - In 'my' world

An Ongoing Encounter

As we have seen this is without doubt an essential experience. But God's Word encourages us to be 'continually filled' (Ephesians 5:18). We are urged to 'walk with' the Holy Spirit (Romans 8:14), and to keep His company (2 Corinthians 13:14).

He becomes the means to our success and the source of our supply.

© Andrew Owen Reprinted 2015 email: dlr@destiny-church.com
Destiny Church, 70 Cathedral Street, Glasgow, G4 0RN
Follow us on Twitter @andrewdestiny @OwenSue @DLR3000   Visit our website www.destinyleadershipresources.com

Study 3

For this Cause

My Personal Notes

For This Cause

Jesus claimed to be a king of a kingdom, and His favourite message was 'The Kingdom of God'.

> '*...The time is fulfilled, and the kingdom of God is at hand. Repent, and believe in the gospel.*'
> Mark 1:15

People who live for a cause are powerfully motivated, and are unlikely to be stopped. Jesus was such a person - He lived for this cause!

> '*You say rightly that I am a king. For this cause I was born, and for this cause I have come into the world...*'
> John 18:37

The Kingdom of God

We may not realise it, but this kingdom changes our lives forever the very moment we decide to follow Jesus. It is powerfully impacting millions all over the world.

> '*He has delivered us from the power of darkness and conveyed us into the kingdom of the Son of His love*'
> Colossians 1:13

Previously, we lived in Satan's kingdom, and promoted his cause. But now we have been set free - not to live our own lives, doing any old thing, but to live for Christ and promote His cause. It truly is a cause worth giving your life for.

The word 'kingdom' means: - 'rule' or 'sovereignty'
                                       - 'will'
                                       - or, 'government'

The 'kingdom' of God therefore, is the place where God's 'will' is done. So, if we have truly come into the kingdom, we will want what God wants.

> '*But seek first the kingdom of God and His righteousness, and all these things shall be added to you.*'
> Matthew 6:33

When you are seeking something first, it means that you will give first priority to it - above every other interest. As believers we are required to put the interests of the 'kingdom' above our own. What God wants must take first call on our time, money, friends, family and future plans. It is the most radical change anyone can experience.

How do we know what the will of God is?

1. He tells us

> *'All Scripture is given by inspiration of God, and is profitable for doctrine, for reproof, for correction, for instruction in righteousness,'*
> 2 Timothy 3:16

The Bible is God's word, full of instructions and promises. The instructions tell us what the will of God is, and how we should live. The promises are the rewards that follow if we do!

These instructions touch every area of our lives - and there is an added bonus - God doesn't just tell us what to do, He also puts the power of the Holy Spirit in us to make us able to do it!

> *'I can do all things through Christ who strengthens me.'*
> Philippians 4:13

What does God think about:

SEX   It's good, and to be enjoyed, but only within hetero-sexual marriage (Ephesians 5:3; Hebrews 13:4)

MONEY   He wants you to have it - but not for it to have you (1 Timothy 6:10; Proverbs 11:25)

TIME   Don't waste it - give God the first part of it (Ecclesiastes 12:1; Ephesians 5:16

FRIENDS   Be a true friend and choose your company well (1 Corinthians 15:33; Proverbs 17:17)

WORK   Work hard, honestly, and with enthusiasm - and God will prosper you (Proverbs 21:5).

MIND   Control it or it will control you (Romans 12:1-2).

© Andrew Owen Reprinted 2015 email: dlr@destiny-church.com
Destiny Church, 70 Cathedral Street, Glasgow, G4 0RN
Follow us on Twitter @andrewdestiny @OwenSue @DLR3000   Visit our website www.destinyleadershipresources.com

BODY   Don't abuse it - look after it. Use it for God. (1 Corinthians 6:19)

CHURCH   Be a part of it and attend regularly (Hebrews 10:25).

BUSINESS   Honour God with it and He will bless you in it (Deuteronomy 8:18).

CITY   God promises that all the families of the earth should be blessed through Abraham and his offspring, that means us and includes our town or city. (Genesis 28:14; 1 Timothy 2:1-2)

FAITH   It's more than a set of beliefs, it's a practical, active lifestyle (James 2:17).

2.   <u>He appoints others to tell us</u>

God will often appoint others to speak for Him. He appoints these delegates as leaders into our lives.

> *'Let every soul be subject to governing authorities. For there is no authority except from God, and the authorities that exist are appointed by God.'*
> Romans 13:1

These delegates are put in place by God: in the world, the home, and the church. While we are never required by God to obey anyone who contradicts God's written word, we are required to listen and obey otherwise.

These delegated authorities are really meant to represent God and make good leadership choices. When they do this, it's great, when they don't - there's trouble.

> *'Righteousness exalts a nation, but sin is a reproach to any people.'*
> Proverbs 14:34

That's why we must pray for them.

> *'... for kings and all who are in authority, that we may lead a quiet and peaceable life in all godliness and reverence.'*
> 1 Timothy 2:2

In the world God appoints: A government over the nations
                              A boss over the company
                              A head over a school
                              (1 Peter 2:13-17)

In the home God appoints: A husband over the marriage
                              A mother and father over the kids
                              (Ephesians 5:22; Ephesians 6:9)

© Andrew Owen Reprinted 2015 email: dlr@destiny-church.com
Destiny Church, 70 Cathedral Street, Glasgow, G4 0RN
Follow us on Twitter @andrewdestiny @OwenSue @DLR3000   Visit our website www.destinyleadershipresources.com

In the church God appoints: Leaders over the congregation (Hebrews 13:17)

We should always positively support leadership, and do all we can to get behind it. Only when they act contrary to the God they are supposed to represent do we have any right to refuse their authority into our lives - and then with the greatest of care.

Motivation

You will only live for a cause if the cause has gripped your heart - and the kingdom life must come out from our hearts. We must have the right attitudes.

Perhaps our attitude can be described as 'our angle of approach to life'. Jesus taught, for example, that anger and hatred are the source of murder and therefore are wrong – even if an act of murder is never committed (Matthew 5:21-24).

In the same message (often called the 'sermon on the mount'), Jesus gave us a list of some of the attitudes we should have, and the rewards that go with them (Matthew 5:3-12).

Kingdom attitudes include:

Desperation — Our utter and total need of God. Jesus described this as being 'poor in spirit'.

Teachability — Jesus used the word 'meek' (not weak!) This means we will allow others to harness our strengths and deal with our weaknesses.

Contending outlook — (Not the same as 'contentious!') An attitude that will strongly reach for all God has, reach for those whom He wants saved, and 'contend' with negative forces in our lives.

Redemptive outlook — We will always respond in mercy and with forgiveness towards others.

Positive expectation — We will always be looking for a great result, for kingdom people are a faith-filled people - they know that this kingdom gets big and successful!

© Andrew Owen Reprinted 2015 email: dlr@destiny-church.com
Destiny Church, 70 Cathedral Street, Glasgow, G4 0RN
Follow us on Twitter @andrewdestiny @OwenSue @DLR3000   Visit our website www.destinyleadershipresources.com

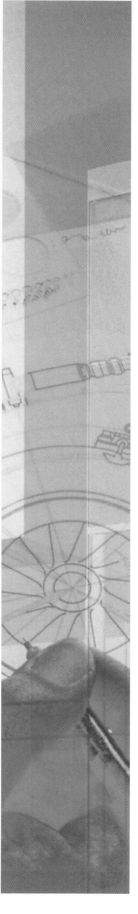

'Of the increase of His government and peace there will be no end, upon the throne of David and over His kingdom, to order it and establish it with judgment and justice from that time forward, even forever.'
Isaiah 9:7

What kind of person do you want to be?

Physically 'we are what we eat', or so they say, and there is a truth spiritually in this also. If the kingdom grips our heart, and we are living for this cause, it will produce within us a kingdom character. You will begin to look like this - because the kingdom looks like this.

1. Strong

'The wicked flee when no one pursues, But the righteous are bold as a lion.'
Proverbs 28:1

You will have an ever increasing inner confidence, knowing that God can do anything, for you, in you, and through you.

2. Passionate

'And from the days of John the Baptist until now the kingdom of heaven suffers violence, and the violent take it by force.'
Matthew 11:12

Passion is a choice, not an emotion. You will refuse to be stopped and will communicate vision and energy into all that you do. The word 'violent' here means in the Greek 'to storm a city'. Passionate people are not passive but active.

3. Flexible

'But we all with unveiled face, beholding as in a mirror the glory of the Lord, are being transformed into the same image from glory to glory, just as by the Spirit of the Lord.'
2 Corinthians 3:18

You cannot become what you are meant to be by remaining what you are. The kingdom means change. If you stop changing, you have stopped growing.

© Andrew Owen Reprinted 2015 email: dlr@destiny-church.com
Destiny Church, 70 Cathedral Street, Glasgow, G4 0RN
Follow us on Twitter @andrewdestiny @OwenSue @DLR3000   Visit our website www.destinyleadershipresources.com

4.　Fruitful

> *that you may walk worthy of the Lord, fully pleasing Him, being fruitful in every good work and increasing in the knowledge of God;'*
> Colossians 1:10

You will be an influence for good, affecting others. You will see results from your endeavours. Jesus said He had called us to be fruitful.

5.　Faithful

> *'And I thank Christ Jesus our Lord who has enabled me, because He counted me faithful, putting me into the ministry,'*
> 1 Timothy 1:12

You will become a reliable, trustworthy person, keeping your word even when it costs you. If necessary you will stand through difficult situations taking comfort that God is with you.

The kingdom of God is the will of God, backed up by His power at work. When I give God first place in my life He will take care of my needs.

6.　Godly

> *'For bodily exercise profits a little, but godliness is profitable for all things, having promise of the life that now is and of that which is to come.'*
> 1 Timothy 4:8

You will have an increasing desire to do things that please God, and stop doing things that displease him.

7.　Relational

> *'to godliness brotherly kindness, and to brotherly kindness love.'*
> 2 Peter 1:7

You will become better at understanding others and giving them space to change. People will be actively involved with your life.

Study 4

The Future

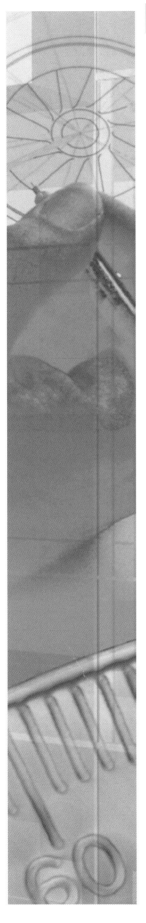

My Personal Notes

© Andrew Owen Reprinted 2015 email: dlr@destiny-church.com
Destiny Church, 70 Cathedral Street, Glasgow, G4 0RN
Follow us on Twitter @andrewdestiny @OwenSue @DLR3000   Visit our website www.destinyleadershipresources.com

The Future

The Bible has a great deal to say about the future, and perhaps today more than ever, people are very concerned about their safety and security.

The Bible introduces us to concepts like:

The last days
The return of Jesus
Resurrection of the dead
Judgement day
Heaven and hell
Eternal life

We read:

> **'...He has put eternity in their hearts...'**
> Ecclesiastes 3:11

> **'Indeed before the day was, I am He; And there is no one who can deliver out of My hand; I work, and who will reverse it?'**
> Isaiah 43:13

We are therefore encouraged to consider these things, and live our lives appropriately. As God has the last word on life, we would do well to heed His advice. If we do, our lives will be filled with hope, peace and victory.

1. The Last Days

> **' ... in _these_ last days he has spoken to us by his Son ...'**
> Hebrews 1:2

This world will not continue for ever! It is running towards an end. God created it (Genesis 1), and God will destroy it (2 Peter 3:10 -12).

The 'last days' or the 'end times' is a frequently referred to theme in scripture. As we see from the above verse, the early Church recognised that they were in the 'last days'. We are therefore now in the 'last of the last days'. History has almost run its course according to God's plan.

The study of things concerning the end times is commonly called 'eschatology'. There are varied views on the sequence of some events, but we will focus on certainties - facts that the Bible makes crystal clear.

a)   The world will end (2 Peter 3:10).

b)   In the last days the world communities will be hallmarked by:

- Great greed

- Rebellion against all authority

- A searching for spirituality but denying God

- Seeking pleasure above all else

        (2 Timothy 3:1-5)

- Much fear

- Many wars

- Increase in world famines

        (Luke 21:26)

- Opposition to the gospel of Christ   (Matthew 24:4)

c)   A massive end time harvest of souls (Micah 4:1), and great opportunity for the Church (Matthew 24:14).

> **'...All over the world this gospel is bearing fruit and _growing_ ...'**
> Colossians 1:6 NIV.

d)   The Church will be mature and attractive.

> **'...Then I John, saw the holy city, New Jerusalem, coming down out of heaven from God, prepared as a bride adorned for her husband'** Revelation 21:2

How To Live In The Last Days!

❖   Prayerfully - keeping watch and guard.

❖   Persistently - don't give up.

❖   Passionately - with hope, faith and energy.

❖   Principled - don't compromise.

❖   Purposefully - with an end in mind.

© Andrew Owen Reprinted 2015 email: dlr@destiny-church.com
Destiny Church, 70 Cathedral Street, Glasgow, G4 0RN
Follow us on Twitter @andrewdestiny @OwenSue @DLR3000   Visit our website www.destinyleadershipresources.com

2. The Return Of Jesus

> *'Men of Galilee, why do you stand gazing up into heaven? This same Jesus, who was taken up from you into heaven, will so come in like manner as you saw Him go into heaven.'*
> Acts 1:11

We are convinced that:

a)   Jesus Christ will return to this world as a mighty conqueror (Revelation 1:7).

b)   He will appear suddenly, without warning (1 Thessalonians 5:2).

c)   His coming will be preceded by a trumpet sound (1 Corinthians 15:52).

d)   His coming will precede the resurrection of the dead and judgement day. (1 Thessalonians 4:16).

3. Resurrection

The resurrection of the dead was a very real and powerful hope in the early church. They:

❖   Realised that their bodies were mortal and one day would die.

❖   Had seen Jesus raised from the dead, with a body that ate, drank, and passed through walls. An indicator of the kind of body we would get.

We believe that at the return of Jesus a great world-wide resurrection will take place. When this message was preached, some found it difficult to believe (Acts 17:32), but the Apostles went on to write convincingly of the truth they had received from Jesus.

1.   Everyone - saved and unsaved, will be raised from the dead (Acts 24:15)

2.   Believers who are still alive when Christ returns will receive an immortal body. (1 Corinthians 15:42-54).

3.   Everyone will have to stand before God at a great throne and face judgement day (Revelation 20:11-15).

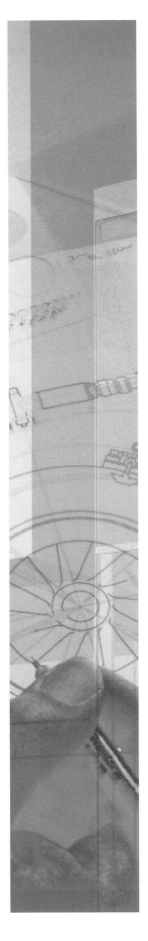

4. Judgement Day

'But we know that the judgment of God is according to truth against those who practice such things.'
Romans 2:2

No-one will escape this day - it is coming! But the Bible makes it clear that the events of that day are influenced by the choices made now!

God is called 'the Judge of all the earth' (Genesis 18:25).

We discover that:

❖ If you are a believer, you have already faced this judgement, the moment you placed your life in Christ. At that point your name was written in the 'Lamb's book of life' (Revelation 21:27).

❖ Believers will face a different judgement (1 Corinthians 3:13-15) - a reward or otherwise for the life they have lived and contribution made for the sake of Christ and His kingdom. God will not be interested in the houses we bought or the cars we drove.

'And behold, I am coming quickly, and My reward is with Me, to give to every one according to his work.'
Revelation 22:12

5. Heaven And Hell

'The soul who sins shall die. The son shall not bear the guilt of the father, nor the father bear the guilt of the son. The righteousness of the righteous shall be upon himself, and the wickedness of the wicked shall be upon himself.'
Ezekiel 18:20

© Andrew Owen Reprinted 2015 email: dlr@destiny-church.com
Destiny Church, 70 Cathedral Street, Glasgow, G4 0RN
Follow us on Twitter @andrewdestiny @OwenSue @DLR3000   Visit our website www.destinyleadershipresources.com

The Bible makes it very clear that the death of the body is not the end of existing, but a doorway to another form of continual existence. <u>But</u>, there is no coming back!

Very often, the fear of dying is actually greater than the fear of death itself – which is assumed to lead to oblivion and a welcome relief from the trials of life. So people take the approach 'eat, drink and be merry, for tomorrow we die', or else they may take the approach that everyone (except the really wicked) goes to heaven. Further we are faced with the very serious ethical questions of euthanasia, mercy killing or assisted suicides. The Bible teaching on eternity challenges all of these ideas.

The Bible teaches us that:

a)   There is conscious existence after death (Luke 16:19-31). The body dies, but the soul continues on.

b)   Today's decisions decide tomorrow's destinations! Once a man dies, his eternal state is decided forever (2 Corinthians 5:10; Luke 16:25).

c)   There is a choice of two destinations: heaven or hell

Heaven:

> *'Indeed heaven and the highest heavens belong to the Lord your God,'*
> Deuteronomy 10:14

The Bible speaks of three heavens:

1st heaven – the atmosphere, polluted by satanic presence (Ephesians 2:2)

2nd heaven – the planets and stars (Genesis 1:15)

3rd heaven – paradise, God's abode (2 Corinthians 12:2-4)

What is it like there?

❖   No more death or pain (Revelation 21:4). You will live forever.

❖   Full of amazing light and glory (Revelation 21:23).

❖   You will have the answer to every question (1 Corinthians 13:8-12).

❖   There will be 'rewards' given for deeds done in the body (2 Corinthians 5:10; Matthew 16:27; Revelation 11:18).

❖   You will be known as you are known, that is - you will be the same person (1 Corinthians 13:12).

Hell:

◆   An actual reality (Matthew 5:22-23).

◆   Was not intended for people, but prepared for the Devil and his angels. Matthew 25:41 has a very serious warning from Jesus himself. It points out that being"good" can still take you to hell. The real issue are who or what are you living for?

◆   Jesus preached passionately against going there (Matthew 10:28; Mark 9:45).

(**Myth**: The Devil is not the lord of hell. It will be his hell.)

When Israel fell into idolatry they went to a valley to burn their children alive to 'Molech' and 'Baal'. Thousands of children were placed on the red hot metal hands of these idols. Their cries were drowned out by frenzied worship. This place was called 'Gehenna'. Later on it became the garbage dump of Jerusalem, with perpetual smouldering fires. This is the imagery that Jesus used to describe hell.

Hell is:

◆   Eternal (2 Thessalonians 1:9)

◆   A lake of fire (Revelation 21:8; Mark 9:43)

◆   Complete darkness (Matthew 8:12)

Hell Will Be Inhabited By:

◆   The Devil (Matthew 25:41)

◆   Fallen angels (2 Peter 2:4)

◆   The unredeemed (Revelation 20:15; Roman 2:5-9)

Where Is The Devil Now?

He is free to roam the earth, seeking those whom he may devour, to influence and seduce.

> *'Be sober, be vigilant; because your adversary the devil walks about like a roaring lion, seeking whom he may devour.'*
> 1 Peter 5:8

Who are these 'whom he may devour'? They are the people who have not come into, or are not living under the authority of God. Keep living under God's rule and you can resist the Devil.

© Andrew Owen Reprinted 2015 email: dlr@destiny-church.com
Destiny Church, 70 Cathedral Street, Glasgow, G4 0RN
Follow us on Twitter @andrewdestiny @OwenSue @DLR3000   Visit our website www.destinyleadershipresources.com

How Does The Devil Influence And Seduce?

1. Temptation (Mark 1:13)
2. Accusation (Revelation 12:9-10)
3. Deception (2 Corinthians 11:3)
4. Oppression (Luke 13:16; Luke 4:18)
5. Attack (2 Timothy 4:18)
6. Possession – but there is no Bible example of Christians being 'possessed'. (Matthew 8:16; Mark 5:1-20)

We should know that:

a) The Devil is a fallen angel (Isaiah 14:12; Revelation 12:7-9)
b) He does not possess Divine attributes – for example he can only be in one place at a time (Matthew 4:11; Job 1:7)
c) He is assisted by other fallen angels (Matthew 12:43-45; Revelation 12:9)
d) He appeals to our fleshly nature – like pride (1John 2:15-17; James 1:14)

Don't open doors that let him devour you!

What Happens When We Die?

Followers of Jesus	Others
Immediately in the presence of God, awaiting a resurrection for life. (2 Corinthians 5:6-8)	Go to hell. There is a gap between them and Heaven (Luke 16:26).

Famous statements like the 'Westminster Confession' put it this way:

'The souls of the righteous being made perfect in holiness are received into the highest heaven where they behold the face of God in light and glory, waiting for the full redemption of their bodies.'

And of the unsaved it says:

'They are cast into hell, where they remain in torment and utter darkness, reserved for the judgment of that great day.'

We should note that access to heaven is <u>only</u> achieved by faith in Jesus!

> **'Nor is there salvation in any other, for there is no other name under heaven given among men by which we must be saved.'**
> Acts 4:12

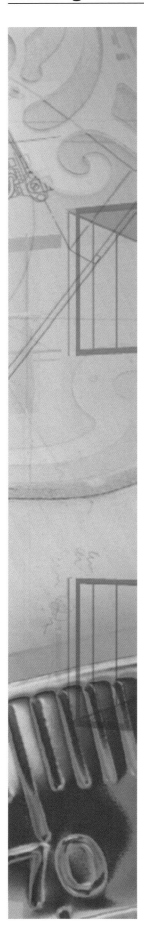

What Should Our Response Be?

Make absolutely sure you are saved

> *'Therefore, my beloved, as you have always obeyed, not as in my presence only, but now much more in my absence, work out your own salvation with fear and trembling;'*
> Philippians 2:12

> *'The only proof of past conversion is present convertedness'*
> J I Packer

Stay faithful. You are personally fully responsible for your own walk with God. You are called to <u>follow</u> Jesus. People should not have to come to chase you.

Prepare your reward, with a fruitful and worthwhile life.

Share your faith with your family, friends and others at every opportunity you get, or they will be lost.

Some say: 'God wouldn't send anyone to hell – he's a God of love'.

What does the Bible say?

- He will keep His word. (Galatians 6:7)

- He does love – by offering you salvation now! He gave His Son so that you don't have to die. (John 3:16)

- God has other attributes – the first name given to God is 'The judge of all the earth' (Genesis 18:25).

> *'And as it is appointed for men to die once, but after this the judgment, [28]so Christ was offered once to bear the sins of many. To those who eagerly wait for Him He will appear a second time, apart from sin, for salvation.*
> Hebrews 9:27-28

© Andrew Owen Reprinted 2015 email: dlr@destiny-church.com
Destiny Church, 70 Cathedral Street, Glasgow, G4 0RN
Follow us on Twitter @andrewdestiny @OwenSue @DLR3000   Visit our website www.destinyleadershipresources.com

Study 5

Planted into the Local Church

© Andrew Owen Reprinted 2015 email: dlr@destiny-church.com
Destiny Church, 70 Cathedral Street, Glasgow, G4 0RN
Follow us on Twitter @andrewdestiny @OwenSue @DLR3000   Visit our website www.destinyleadershipresources.com

My Personal Notes

© Andrew Owen Reprinted 2015 email: dlr@destiny-church.com
Destiny Church, 70 Cathedral Street, Glasgow, G4 0RN
Follow us on Twitter @andrewdestiny @OwenSue @DLR3000   Visit our website www.destinyleadershipresources.com

Planted into the Local Church

We have continued to point out the importance of building our lives 'according to the pattern'. Jesus taught most earnestly the importance of having personal foundations; the man who took pains with those things, He said, was like a man who built his house on the rock. The concept of building is used again, only now we talk about the Church.

> *'Those who are planted in the house of the Lord shall flourish in the courts of our God.'*
> Psalm 92:13

> *'in whom you also are being built together for a dwelling place of God in the Spirit.'*
> Ephesians 2:22

He also said:

> *'I will build My church,'*
> Matthew 16:18

Jesus had a very clear intention – That we live our lives as fully functioning members of a local church.

What is The Church?

It is clear from scripture that not everything that calls itself 'church' is Church. We need to look again at what the Bible says. There are two Greek words that are usually used and translated as 'church', the first of which is:

A)   EKKLESIA

Definition: 'summoned ones', usually translated 'assembly' or 'congregation'.

◆   Ekklesia means 'a summoned people'. There is a clear sense of ownership and purpose. The 'ekklesia' are God's people, called by Him, to listen to what He has to say and to do what He asks.

◆   Ekklesia also has a Greek background. In the great days of classical Greece, great cities like Athens had an 'ekklesia'. It was a counsel that consisted of all the people who had the right of citizenship. They would come together and direct the affairs of the city and their powers were almost unlimited. They could declare war, contract treaties, elect generals, and they were ultimately responsible for the conduct of all military operations. The ekklesia was a summons for every man to come, not only to enjoy the privileges of being a part but also a call to shoulder responsibility.

© Andrew Owen Reprinted 2015 email: dlr@destiny-church.com
Destiny Church, 70 Cathedral Street, Glasgow, G4 0RN
Follow us on Twitter @andrewdestiny @OwenSue @DLR3000   Visit our website www.destinyleadershipresources.com **55**

His Church

In the light of this information, it is interesting that the same word is used for God's 'ekklesia'. The Church should be moving in that same frame of reference! God's ekklesia should be moving in power and authority, directing the affairs of the world and really seeing His kingdom rule come. God's ekklesia are those He is summoning together to hear HIS Word and do HIS will with the power HE has provided. This comes as a surprise to some who have seen the Church as something weak and ineffective. It is a call for us all not only to enjoy the privileges of belonging, but to shoulder our responsibilities as well. The Church is God's house. We should note:

1.　It is His – and He designs it
2.　It should be an effective witness and a powerful influence
3.　It should represent God's character, nature, and purpose

Who is Part of This Church?

As we have already said, not everything that calls itself 'church' is Church. We have become accustomed to the Church being thought of as anyone who attends a building, or even the building itself! In God's eyes the Church is PEOPLE, but not all people. As far as God is concerned there are only two groups of people in the world: those who have acknowledged Jesus as Lord and received eternal life, and those who still remain in the kingdom of darkness and are still spiritually dead. 'Going to church' for that person is no more than dressing a corpse.

Ekklesia can mean:

a)　Universal Church: (Ephesians 1:22-23)

This is the Church to which every believer belongs. It is world-wide and spans the ages.

b)　Local Church: (Romans 16:1; 1 Corinthians 1:2)

This is the 'on the ground' expression in each locality of God's ekklesia. You are to belong to both!

Being part of a local church does not necessarily mean being part of a church in your village or street. You should be a part of a local living church. Sometimes we say - A church alive is worth the drive!

© Andrew Owen Reprinted 2015 email: dlr@destiny-church.com
Destiny Church, 70 Cathedral Street, Glasgow, G4 0RN
Follow us on Twitter @andrewdestiny @OwenSue @DLR3000　Visit our website www.destinyleadershipresources.com

We will now turn our attention to the second word that is used for church:

B) KOINONIA

Definition: 'fellowship'.

The Greek word translated 'fellowship' is one of the most beautiful words in the New Testament. It describes a partnership where people come together and share life. The essential meaning of the word is 'TOGETHERNESS'. It includes:

❖   To **have** shared in something   (common experience)
❖   To **have a** share in something (common possession)
❖   To **want to** share in something(common vision)

The Koinonia Lifestyle

a)   Common experience

We all come from different backgrounds but really we are all alike. We have the same needs, and need the same experience. The experience we all share is that we have received of Jesus' eternal life.

> *'The cup of blessing which we bless, is it not the communion of the blood of Christ? The bread which we break, is it not the communion of the body of Christ?'*
> 1 Corinthians 10:16

Jesus spoke of Himself as being the key, the rock on which the Church would be built. We are not together because of our colour, culture, age, or any other thing when we come to the Church, we will meet a new culture and should be willing to change some things we may be used to. It's a kingdom culture.

b)   Common Possession

> *'Now all who believed were together, and had all things in common.'*
> Acts 2:44

This does not mean that they lived communally, but that they were willing to make available to each other whatever they had. They had a vested interest in each other's welfare. They applied this principle materially and spiritually.

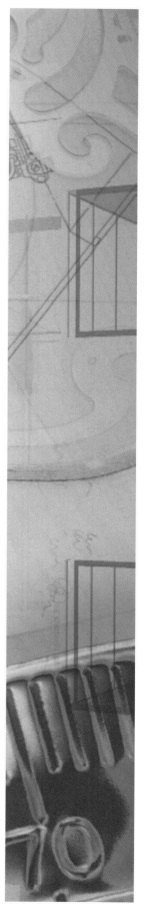

'from whom the whole body, joined and knit together by what every joint supplies, according to the effective working by which every part does its share, causes growth of the body for the edifying of itself in love.'
Ephesians 4:16

c)   Common Vision

If we reflect back to the use of the word 'church' in classical Greece, we will realise that the Church is meant to be a very powerful and influential force. We have a common objective – to enjoy God, and reach this world for Jesus. We must therefore:

i)   Participate in the gospel (Philippians 1:5-7).

We should be witnesses ourselves and support others in their efforts. We can do this by:

❖   Praying (Colossians 4:3)
❖   Giving (2 Corinthians 8:9)
❖   Going (Matthew 9:37-38)
❖   Bringing (John 4:39-40)

ii)   Supply in the church (Ephesians 4:16):

❖   Your presence (Hebrews 10:25)
❖   Yourself - time/gifts/talents (Romans 12:1-2)
❖   Your money (Malachi 3:8-12)
❖   Your faith (1 Thessalonians 1:8)

ii)   Have social significance:

❖   Be an effective witness in your workplace
❖   Don't isolate yourself from the world
❖   Provide relevant answers for today's challenging issues
❖   Live an affirming lifestyle as a good testimony
❖   Get involved with social change as God leads and according to the gifts and passions you have - this may mean serving in a mercy ministry or being a voice on an issue

© Andrew Owen Reprinted 2015 email: dlr@destiny-church.com
Destiny Church, 70 Cathedral Street, Glasgow, G4 0RN
Follow us on Twitter @andrewdestiny @OwenSue @DLR3000   Visit our website www.destinyleadershipresources.com

LIVING A COVENANT LIFE

This condition of 'TOGETHERNESS' would naturally be impossible. There are too many things that would pull it apart. The Devil has a good try – he's called the accuser of the brethren but in many places he doesn't have to bother because foolish Christians do the job for him through complaining or being negative about their church or the people in it. However, the Church of Jesus Christ is not a natural structure, but supernatural, and it is established on a COVENANT that God has made with us. Again and again the Bible emphasises the 'covenant-keeping' nature of God. The Church is a 'covenant community'; we stick together through thick and thin.

> *'A man who has friends must himself be friendly, But there is a friend who sticks closer than a brother.'*
> Proverbs 18:24

Covenant is an important word; it means a 'binding contract between two parties'. The covenant that we have with God is amazing because He instigated it. There was nothing that we could offer Him in the deal, yet He chose to give to us. This covenant has been established through the blood of Christ – it is a blood covenant. Covenants always include conditions that have to be met by each party. The covenant that God has made with us is filled with precious promises.

They include:

❖ Forgiveness of sins (1John 1:9)
❖ Healing (James 5:14-15)
❖ Provision (Philippians 4:19)
❖ Protection (Psalm 91)
❖ presence (Matthew 28:20)

We, equally, have to keep covenant with God. This, according to the NT is very simply put into two requirements. Love God with all your heart-and then your neighbour as yourself. Matthew 22:36-39. Living it out in practical ways includes-

❖ Being faithful to Him (Revelation 2:10; 14:12)
❖ Fulfilling our service (Luke 12:35; Ephesians 4:11-16; Romans 12:1)
❖ Giving of our finances (2 Corinthians 9:7-8)
❖ Keeping covenant with each other (Philippians 2:1-4)
❖ Honouring leadership (Hebrews 13:7,17)

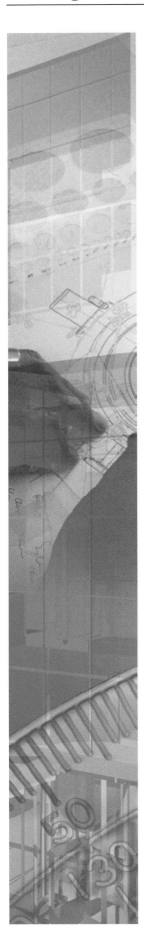

The Church was never brought to birth by God for defensive purposes; it was initiated by Him for advance. God's Church is the vehicle of God's kingdom. It is a nursery school, college and family firm that births, equips and trains God's people to play their role in changing the world and extending God's kingdom. It must become a voice for righteousness and justice, for His ultimate glory and the benefit of mankind.

Why You Must Be Part Of A Local Living Church

Jesus loves the Church passionately

> *'Husbands, love your wives, just as Christ also loved the church and gave Himself for her,'*
> Ephesians 5:25

He wants you in it!

> *'In whom you also are being built together for a dwelling place of God in the Spirit.'*
> Ephesians 2:22

You are uniquely gifted to help its growth

> *'from whom the whole body, joined and knit together by what every joint supplies, according to the effective working by which every part does its share, causes growth of the body for the edifying of itself in love.'*
> Ephesians 4:16

You will be helped there

> *'May He send you help from the sanctuary, And strengthen you out of Zion;'*
> Psalm 20:2

You will prosper when you are planted in it

> *'Those who are planted in the house of the Lord Shall flourish in the courts of our God.'*
> Psalm 92:13

You will be brought to maturity there

> *'Him we preach, warning every man and teaching every man in all wisdom, that we may present every man perfect in Christ Jesus.'*
> Colossians 1:28

You will be empowered there

> *'For the equipping of the saints for the work of ministry, for the edifying of the body of Christ,'*
> Ephesians 4:12

© Andrew Owen Reprinted 2015 email: dlr@destiny-church.com
Destiny Church, 70 Cathedral Street, Glasgow, G4 0RN
Follow us on Twitter @andrewdestiny @OwenSue @DLR3000   Visit our website www.destinyleadershipresources.com

It can lead to a strong, peaceful life

> *'"The glory of this latter temple shall be greater than the former", says the Lord of hosts. "And in this place I will give peace,"' says the Lord of hosts.'*
> Haggai 2:9

The Church Should Be:

a)   A family (Matthew 6:9) – where we belong.

b)   A body (1 Corinthians 12:27) – where we function and play our part.

c)   A healing river (1 Corinthians 12:9; Ezekiel 47:9) – where we take God's life into the community.

d)   An army (2 Timothy 2:3) – where we push back the powers of darkness.

e)   A house (Ephesians 2:22) – where God feels at home, and it looks amazing.

f)   A city (Revelation 21:2) – that provides protection and a different, better lifestyle.

g)   A mountain (Isaiah 2:3) – that cannot be missed, and raises everyone to a higher level. AND whatever we do in it-is done with STRENGTH. We do it STRONG.

h)   A bride (Revelation 21:2) – who is passionately in love with Jesus.

How Do I Get Involved?

1.   Come every week to the church celebrations.

2.   Get connected to the small group system, attend a living cell.

3.   Build friendships through being hospitable and friendly.

4.   Involve with the programme by supporting with your presence, availability and ability.

5.   Find a place to serve and give out from what God has given you. Become a part of a functioning team.

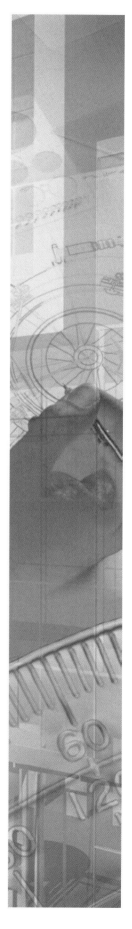

My Personal Notes

Study 6

The Prosperous Life

My Personal Notes

The Prosperous Life - Be Blessed!

Throughout the scripture, poverty is viewed as a curse and prosperity as a blessing. **God wants you to prosper.**

We are never offered 'poverty' as a reward for following the Lord, but we are offered prosperity.

> *'He shall be like a tree planted by the rivers of water, that brings forth its fruit in its season, whose leaf also shall not wither; and whatever he does shall prosper.'*
> Psalm 1:3

Many of us were in poverty when God found us, but He doesn't want us to stay there.

> *'Beloved, I pray that in all respects you may prosper and be in good health, just as your soul prospers.'*
> 3 John 2 NASB

God's thinking of prosperity is to be in a place where you have everything you need and more besides to give away.

You <u>need</u> to prosper for the sake of God's house.

> *'Because of the house of the Lord our God I will seek your good.'*
> Psalm 122:9

It is not appropriate to think 'as long as my needs are met I'm happy', when there is a world to win! You need to be blessed to be a blessing - not just so that you can have more, but to enable you to give more! Getting to this place of abundance is usually a journey for most of us, but it is a journey we should begin, determined to follow God's plan to get there.

> *'You make a living by what you get, you make a life by what you give.'*

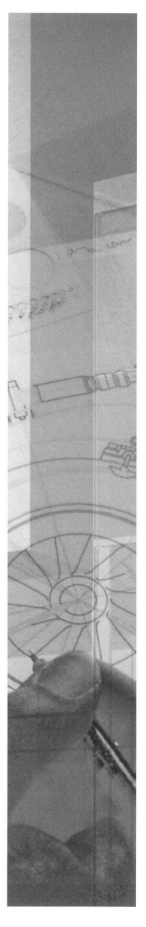

© Andrew Owen Reprinted 2015 email: dlr@destiny-church.com
Destiny Church, 70 Cathedral Street, Glasgow, G4 0RN
Follow us on Twitter @andrewdestiny @OwenSue @DLR3000   Visit our website www.destinyleadershipresources.com

Money has become a taboo subject in many Christian circles; yet according to the scriptures it is an important issue. One source points out that:

◈ One in every four verses in Matthew, Mark and Luke deals with money.

◈ One in every six verses in the New Testament makes reference to money.

◈ Almost half of the parables told by Jesus included money or its misuse.

◈ The only disciple to fall away (Judas) fell over money (John 12:4-8; Acts 1:25).

Be Warned!

> *'For the love of money is a root of all kinds of evil,'*
> 1 Timothy 6:10

The coveting of money or material possessions is sinful, and ends in our hurt and the hurt of others (Luke 12:16-21; Exodus 20:17). It can lead to serious debt problems.

To sell your life for material gains is foolish; you can take nothing with you.

Don't think that it's only people who are covetous or greedy who have a problem with money, for many times 'stingy' or 'mean' people have the greatest problem (Proverbs 11:24-25)

Money in itself is neither good nor bad. However, money can and should be used for good. You need money to live, and you need money to give.

What Does The Bible Teach About Wealth?

1. **God owns it all**

   > *'The earth is the Lord's, and all its fullness, The world and those who dwell therein.'*
   > Psalm 24:1

2. **The power to create it is in His hands** and He gives that power to whom He chooses (Deuteronomy 8:18).

3. **Seek a greater treasure first** and then these other things will come! (Matthew 6:20; Matthew 6:33)

4. **When you end up with it, be very careful it doesn't have you!** (Deuteronomy 8:17-18)

What Is God's Financial Plan For Me?

1.　To provide for me all I need.

　　'And my God shall supply all your need according to His riches in glory by Christ Jesus.'
　　Philippians 4:19

2.　To make me a blessing to others. (Luke 6:38) This could mean giving to others, or how about employing others?

3.　To take me out of poverty.

4.　To make me a financial resourcer of His house the Church, and a financial provider for the proclamation of the gospel. (Malachi 3:10)

5.　To enable me to provide for my family.

　　'I have been young, and now am old; yet I have not seen the righteous forsaken, nor his descendants begging bread.'
　　Psalm 37:25

God's Economy Works Through Exchange!

God's way of working with people is to draw their involvement and participation. He usually gives to us in SEED FORM.

　　'Now may He who supplies seed to the sower, and bread for food, supply and multiply the seed you have sown and increase the fruits of your righteousness.'
　　2 Corinthians 9:10

We then, have to sow the seed in order to reap the harvest.

Sometimes Costly

　　'Those who sow in tears Shall reap in joy. He who continually goes forth weeping, Bearing seed for sowing, Shall doubtless come again with rejoicing, Bringing his sheaves with him.'
　　Psalm 126:5-6

The Old Testament Israelites on returning from years in exile had little. The wife and mother would, under pressure, think 'we cannot sow –we must eat'; with tears she would hold back her husband. He might have replied 'if we do not sow now – we will not reap then'. Sowing and reaping is a God ordained principle that always works.

> **'Do not be deceived, God is not mocked; for whatever a man sows, that he will also reap.'**
> Galatians 6:7

The way you handle your money says a lot about you. How you spend your money is how you spend your life.

6 Things We Are Encouraged To Do With Money

1. Tithe On Everything You Receive

> **'Bring all the tithes into the storehouse, That there may be food in My house, And try Me now in this, Says the Lord of hosts, If I will not open for you the windows of heaven And pour out for you such blessing That there will not be room enough to receive it.'**
> Malachi 3:10

The Bible teaches that we bring our tithes. We do not <u>give</u> our tithes as they are God's anyway! Tithe simply means one tenth. In recognizing God as our source we bring our tithes.

Tithing is for all believers:
It is not only for wage-earners; from the youngest to the oldest, all ought to tithe.

Storehouse tithing:
The tithe is not yours to do as you please with, but should go into the storehouse. The storehouse is the place from which you are fed, led and nurtured. The storehouse is the local church

We tithe as regularly as we receive:
Your <u>income</u> does not come from your work, government or grant, it comes <u>from</u> God, <u>through</u> your employer.

Tithing With Expectation:
Malachi 3:10 is the only place in the Bible where we are invited to put God to the test. He promises to 'open the windows of heaven' and 'rebuke the devourer'.

Tithing Is Found Throughout The Entire Bible

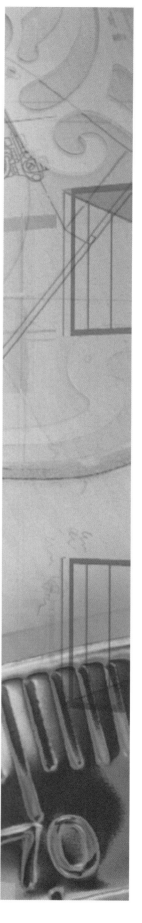

❖   Tithing was practiced before the giving of the law by Abraham (Genesis 14:20).

❖   Tithing was included in the Levitical laws (Numbers 18:21).

❖   Tithing was endorsed by the prophets (Malachi 3:8).

❖   Tithing was endorsed by Jesus

   'These you ought to have done, without leaving the others undone.'
   Matthew 23:23

❖   Abraham is held up as our example (Hebrews 7:4)

If we hold back from releasing that which belongs to God – we will lose it anyway! (Matthew 10:39).

2.   Give Offerings Over And Above Your Tithes

We start giving after we have brought our tithes. These are our freewill offering. Concerning offerings, the Bible teaches:

❖   They are as important as tithing and should be regularly practiced (Malachi 3:8).

❖   They should be given with faith, and cheerfully (2 Corinthians 9:6-7)

❖   They should be given regularly in a prepared way (1 Corinthians 16:2)

3.   Have A Generous Outlook In Life

a)   Having first brought our tithes and secondly given our offerings, we also have an instruction to give where there is need, especially to those of the household of faith (James 2:14-17).

'Therefore, as we have opportunity, let us do good to all, especially to those who are of the household of faith.'
Galatians 6:10

b)   Share with your teachers

'Let him who is taught the word share in all good things with him who teaches.'
Galatians 6:6

Spiritual truth causes physical and material prosperity. Share and sow back into the lives of those who teach you the word.

4.   Exercise Faith Strongly To Believe God For A Return

5.   Always Be A Good <u>Steward</u>!

A steward is a person who manages that which belongs to another. Being a good steward means that:

i)   You will realize that all you have is truly God's and not yours.

'For you were bought at a price; therefore glorify God in your body and in your spirit, which are God's.'
1 Corinthians 6:20

ii)   You will manage it to the best of your ability for the <u>benefit</u> of the owner.

iii)   You will have to give an account to the owner (God) for your stewardship (Luke 16:1-13).

6.   Work Hard And Be Industrious
(Proverbs 31:10-31)

7.   Be Patient (Galatians 6:9)

© Andrew Owen Reprinted 2015 email: dlr@destiny-church.com
Destiny Church, 70 Cathedral Street, Glasgow, G4 0RN
Follow us on Twitter @andrewdestiny @OwenSue @DLR3000   Visit our website www.destinyleadershipresources.com

Handling Finance In The Church

The way we handle our finances has a direct bearing on our promotion and influence.

> **'Therefore if you have not been faithful in the unrighteous mammon, who will commit to your trust the true riches? And if you have not been faithful in what is another man's, who will give you what is your own?**
> Luke 16:11-12

When God sees that we handle our material things well, He will entrust us with more, especially things that really matter, like reaching others and changing cities.

The church should be exemplary in it's financial management. Not just complying with the laws of the land, but stewarding to the highest standards.

Whilst the church appointed leaders are responsible for this task, they will often create a finance team to assist them. This is a very important team in the life of the church. Good protocol should be put in place for these teams to follow. Your local church leadership should be more than happy to tell you how it works.

Further, we should be wise with our financial management. In many countries governments assist churches and charities through tax return schemes. Where these exist we should maximise their potential.
Many people plan ahead-have you thought about your church in your legacy and will?

It has also become the practice of many business people, to not only personally give. but to give out of their company profits. Setting a great example for others to follow.

My Personal Notes

Study 7

Win-Some Ways

My Personal Notes

Win-Some Ways

We were created needing each other, but all too often we hurt each other.

So many have found that getting too close has only produced pain and disappointment - perhaps the traumas of divorce or abuse. The old saying is true: 'hurt people, hurt people'. Consequently the cycle of broken relationships continues. However, it doesn't have to be that way, and the Bible promises that God will:

> *'...turn The hearts of the fathers to the children,*
> *And the hearts of the children to their fathers...'*
> Malachi 4:6

Further, relationships and alliances can be powerful forces used as keys to promote some amazing things.
We as believers need to learn how to make, keep and produce relationships that promote Christ and His kingdom. As a result we will see positive benefits in our lives. This takes some skill and understanding.

We learn from the Bible that:

> *'...he who wins souls is wise.'*
> Proverbs 11:30

1. Relationships Affect Us

    a)   Our health (1 Corinthians 11:30)
    b)   Our prayers (1 Peter 3:7)
    c)   Our help and assistance (Proverbs 17:17)
    d)   Our prosperity (Ecclesiastes 4:9)
    e)   Our maturity (Ephesians 5:21)
    f)   Our greater effectiveness (Ephesians 4:16)

2. Not All Relationships Are Equal

Some relationships are to be more intimate than others.

If I understand this I will:

a) Give time to:

    1.   God
    2.   My marriage
    3.   My children
    4.   My church
    5.   My unsaved family, friends and colleagues

For my relationships to work, I have to know how to love with God's love. (1 Corinthians 13).

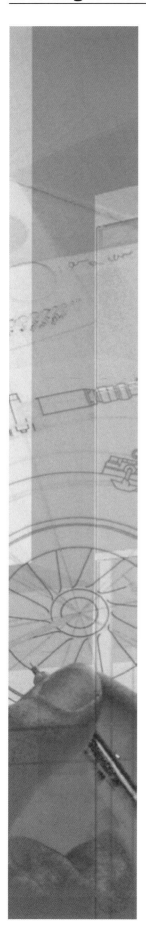

b)　Have the right expectations

I should measure my expectations so that I do not get disappointed or disappoint others. Those who follow Jesus' teachings will have a different value system placed in their lives to those who do not.

3.　All My Relationships Have A Purpose

a)　To win others (1 Corinthians 9:19).
b)　To influence others (1 Thessalonians 4:12).
c)　To help others (Titus 3:8).
d)　To keep others (Matthew 5:24).
e)　To make up what's lacking in me (1 Corinthians 12:21).
f)　To enrich my life (1 Corinthians 12:21).
g)　To build a better world (Proverbs 14:24).
h)　To fulfill God's ultimate goal (Revelation 5:9).

I need to be a relational person.

4.　To Build Good Relationships There Must Be Rules of Engagement

Because I am subject to continuous change, and because my world can be in constant flux, I have to build my relationships like a good house - on solid foundations! These foundations have to be strong, certain and unshakeable. They are the 'rules of engagement'.

Marriage is a good example. When a couple gets married each make their vows to the other, which the law recognizes as a legally binding agreement. These vows are their 'rules of engagement'. They have rights, privileges and expectations which they then must live by, and with God and the church's encouragement - they can.

© Andrew Owen Reprinted 2015 email: dlr@destiny-church.com
Destiny Church, 70 Cathedral Street, Glasgow, G4 0RN
Follow us on Twitter @andrewdestiny @OwenSue @DLR3000   Visit our website www.destinyleadershipresources.com

a)   Covenant - God's rules of engagement

The Bible describes God as a 'covenant-keeping God' (Deuteronomy 7:9). Covenant is another word for 'contract' or 'agreement'. While we cannot expect the world to live like this, God throws open an invitation for you to enter into this agreement with Him and then both shoulder the responsibility it offers, and enjoy the rewards it gives. Since God keeps His word, He will never break the relationship with us.

> **'... I will not leave you nor forsake you.'**
> Joshua 1:5

b)   A community with great purpose and high expectations

Wedding rings are frequently used as a token and memory of our marriage vows. Likewise, Jesus instigated a tradition that He wishes us to remember Him and this covenant by.

We call this 'communion' or 'the Lord's table'.

> **'and when He had given thanks, He broke it and said, "Take, eat; this is My body which is broken for you; do this in remembrance of Me.'**
> 1 Corinthians 11:24-25

This demonstrated the importance of the Body and good healthy relationships inside it! He also expects us to attach the same importance to it and to each other. Every effort should be made to build relationships with people who are pursuing the same purpose as yourself. You should prioritise your relationships to this end!

Communion

When we break bread we should:

i)   Know that it is a 'Believers only' event.

ii)   You should always break bread with at least one other believer.

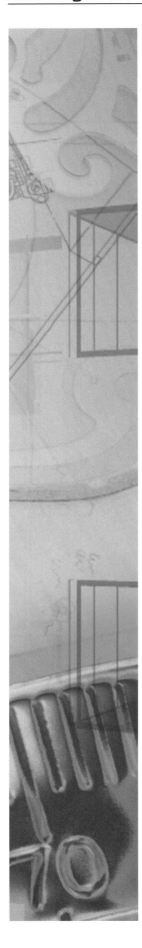

iii) Examine ourselves. There should be nothing between us and God.

iv) Discern the Lord's body. This speaks of the Church. Never break bread if you carry a problem between yourself and another believer – it could have serious consequences. You could become sick, or even die.

v) Remember the Lord's death. It provided not only forgiveness for sin, but deliverance from its consequences – including sickness.

vi) Until He comes. It is not a sad meal, but a happy one. There will also be a time when this comes to an end at the return of the Lord.

c)　God expects us to

1. Love one another (John 13:34)
2. Look after each other's welfare (1 Corinthians 10:24)
3. Don't judge each other (James 4:12)
4. Be of one mind – this is a command (Philippians 1:27)
5. Labour together (Philippians 1:27)
6. Serve one another (John 13:14)
7. Prefer each other (Romans 12:10)
8. Admonish each other in love (Romans 15:14)
9. Greet each other with warmth (Romans 16:16)
10. Carry each other's burdens (Galatians 6:2)
11. Submit to each other (Ephesians 5:21)
12. Speak the truth to each other (Ephesians 4:15)
13. Don't gossip about each other (James 4:11)
14. Don't bear grudges (James 5:9)
15. Confess your faults (James 5:16)
16. Pray for one another (James 5:16)
17. Be hospitable (1 Peter 4:9)
18. Fellowship with each other (1 John 1:7)
19. Be at peace with your brother (Mark 9:50)
20. Receive each other – no cliques! (Romans 15:7)
21. Be kind to each other, tender – not harsh (Ephesians 4:32)
22. Forbear, or have patience (Ephesians 4:2)

How would you score on a scale of 1-10 on the above points?

© Andrew Owen Reprinted 2015 email: dlr@destiny-church.com
Destiny Church, 70 Cathedral Street, Glasgow, G4 0RN
Follow us on Twitter @andrewdestiny @OwenSue @DLR3000   Visit our website www.destinyleadershipresources.com

5. We Must Cultivate Covenant Keeping

Keeping covenant has great advantages:

❖　You are pleasing God, as His word commands it

❖　It will keep you in good harmony with the rest of the church and in good health

❖　It will be a major contributing factor in receiving God's blessing on the church

> *'Behold, how good and how pleasant it is For brethren to dwell together in unity! … For there the Lord commanded the blessing – Life forevermore.'*
> Psalm 133

When we look at scripture we can quickly deduce that it is God who gives growth in the church.

> *'I planted, Apollos watered, but God gave the increase. So then neither he who plants is anything, nor he who waters, but God who gives the increase.'*
> 1 Corinthians 3:6-7

While 'blessing, growth and increase' is the prayer of many, we need to understand that God's blessings fall in certain places.

Read Psalm 133.

God holds in the highest esteem the <u>unity</u> of believers.

> *'endeavoring to keep the unity of the Spirit in the bond of peace.'*
> Ephesians 4:3

While there is great personal enjoyment from good relationships, the purposes of God must be the things that have the greatest attention in our lives. We must be Christ-centred, then, together, we become a winning team!

While we all want to belong, we do not allow the need for intimacy to keep the church small, as others must be reached. These different needs for mission and family are <u>not</u> conflicting, but complimentary.

6. How Do I Build And Keep Good Relationships?

a) Be a peacemaker, not a peacekeeper

> *'Blessed are the peacemakers, For they shall be called sons of God.'*
> Matthew 5:9

Sometimes, where there is a problem, people clam up and say nothing – they think 'let's keep the peace'. We, however, have to be peacemakers, which sometimes means conflict, discussion and dialogue. This way true lasting peace emerges.

b) Accept Personal Responsibility

> *'Therefore if you bring your gift to the altar, and there remember that your brother has something against you, leave your gift there before the altar, and go your way. First be reconciled to your brother, and then come and offer your gift.'*
> Matthew 5:23-24

> *'Moreover if your brother sins against you, go and tell him his fault between you and him alone. If he hears you, you have gained your brother.'*
> Matthew 18:15

Both these texts show us that, whenever there is a breakdown in relationship, the responsibility lies with US to put things right.

c) Refuse to be Offended

> *A brother offended is harder to win than a strong city, And contentions are like the bars of a castle.*
> Proverbs 18:19

Everyone has an opportunity to be offended. The Greek New Testament word for 'offence' is 'skandalizo, which means to put a 'snare in a trap' or a 'stumbling block' in the way. Don't fall for the bait, refuse to be offended.

© Andrew Owen Reprinted 2015 email: dlr@destiny-church.com
Destiny Church, 70 Cathedral Street, Glasgow, G4 0RN
Follow us on Twitter @andrewdestiny @OwenSue @DLR3000   Visit our website www.destinyleadershipresources.com

7. Consider These Helpful Steps

a) Your aim should always be to be reconciled to your brother, not to win the argument. The Bible emphasises speaking the truth in LOVE. Live with a <u>redemptive</u> attitude.

b) Try to understand before pressing to be understood.

c) You have two ears and one mouth – twice as much listening as talking!

c) Always come out of a place of peace, never of reaction.

d) Never be afraid of confrontation.

e) The circle of restitution needs to be as large as the circle of offence.

f) Be quick to forgive and forget.

g) Whenever possible try to speak face to face.

h) Deal as quickly as possible with unresolved issues.

i) It is never enough to say 'sorry'. We must ask for forgiveness. This way the onus is placed on the other party to forgive. We have then fully played our part.

j) Refuse to gossip and refuse to be involved in negative, unhealthy conversations about others.

'Commitment is laying down the right to quit'.
C J Mahoney

My Personal Notes

Study 8

Two Great Commandments

My Personal Notes

Two Great Commandments

Jesus was once asked what He considered to be the most important principles. He replied:

> ' …*"You shall love the Lord your God with all your heart, with all your soul, and with all your mind.'* This is the first and great commandment. And the second is like it: 'You shall love your neighbour as yourself.'"*
>
> Matthew 22:36-39

Pretty straightforward and clear, but easier said than done. All too often our love for God is shallow. It is often measured in direct proportion to the 'blessings' and 'favours' we may feel we get from Him. Our commitment to love others is often also high on intention and low on action. But when we do have a genuine, bona-fide experience with God, He does change our hearts.

> *'For Christ's love compels us…'*
>
> 2 Corinthians 5:14, NIV

The more we get to know Him, the more we change. Having then become convinced that we should love God, and love others passionately, we need to learn and understand how we can do that. How can we then turn our intention into reality?

> *'Now for this very reason also, applying all diligence, in your faith supply moral excellence, and in your moral excellence, knowledge; and in your knowledge, self-control, and in your self-control, perseverance, and in your perseverance, godliness; and in your godliness, brotherly kindness, and in your brotherly kindness, love.'*
>
> 2 Peter 1:5-7, NASB

It is true that we do not exist for ourselves, but for the benefit of those not yet with us.

God's kind of love works like this:

1. From The Inside Out

Most religions work from the outside in. If we can do things right on the outside perhaps we will find happiness on the inside. But knowing Christ is different, He changes our hearts!

> *'…I will put My law in their minds, and write it on their hearts…'*
>
> Jeremiah 31:33

Destiny Church, 70 Cathedral Street, Glasgow, G4 0RN
Follow us on Twitter @andrewdestiny @OwenSue @DLR3000   Visit our website www.destinyleadershipresources.com

a)　Fruits of the Spirit

'But the fruit of the Spirit is love, joy, peace, longsuffering, kindness, goodness, faithfulness, gentleness, self-control. Against such there is no law.'
Galatians 5:22-23

These qualities are described as fruit produced by a supernatural God at work in our lives. They then become part of our character and enable us to live out the great commandments. Just as the fruit of a tree is not intended for the tree to eat, but for the benefit of others, so others benefit from these fruits in our lives. The fruit feeds relationship and lubricates the friendship.

b)　The Greatest Thing is Love

'And now abide faith, hope, love, these three; but the greatest of these is love.'
1 Corinthians 13:13

God himself is defined as 'love' (1 John 4:8; 1 John 4:16). When the Greek New Testament was written, there were two commonly used words for love:

'Eros':　　Sexual, lustful, sensual love

'Phileo':　Brotherly kindness

But a new, stronger, different word was coined for God's kind of love:

'Agape':　This is an unselfish love, looking for nothing in return. It is a love that just wants to give.

We can take comfort from understanding that this is the kind of love with which God loves us. He just wants to give!

'For God so loved the world that He gave His only begotten Son...'
John 3:16

Although people can genuinely love each other, God's love has a unique distinguishing feature; it can love the 'unlovely', 'undeserving' or the 'unknown'.

© Andrew Owen Reprinted 2015 email: dlr@destiny-church.com
Destiny Church, 70 Cathedral Street, Glasgow, G4 0RN
Follow us on Twitter @andrewdestiny @OwenSue @DLR3000　Visit our website www.destinyleadershipresources.com

2. Love Is A Priority

As we have been commanded to love God, and love our neighbour, we must give our lives to the development of a love-filled lifestyle and take positive steps in our lives to maximise its impact.

a)   Love Is Seen

Love is not just an emotion, but is a lifestyle that can be seen by the things it does (1 Corinthians 13). Love is always practical. It looks for opportunities to <u>do</u> something. To love is a <u>choice</u>.

b)   Loving My Neighbour

'Who is my neighbour?' was a question put to Jesus in Luke 10:29. At this point we get the story of the good Samaritan.

We learn from this story that 'your neighbour' is <u>not</u> the person most like you, or even living next door to you. Your neighbour is the person <u>most</u> unlike you, from another people group. Traditionally Jews and Samaritans didn't talk to each other, but this dividing line was crossed because the Samaritan chose to love his neighbour.

This may mean: Young loving old
Black loving white
Churched loving un-churched
Straight loving gay
Christian loving Muslim

We also see that 'neighbour' is anyone who is in need. I am duty bound to help them.

> *'Find a hurt and heal it, find a need and meet it.'*

It is easy to love our friend who loves us back, but God's kind of love is bigger than that.

3. Powerful Love

When we love like God loves, we will act like God acts. So many times before Jesus performed a miracle we read:

> *'Then Jesus, moved with <u>compassion</u>, stretched out His hand and touched him... immediately the leprosy left him...'*
> Mark 1:41-42

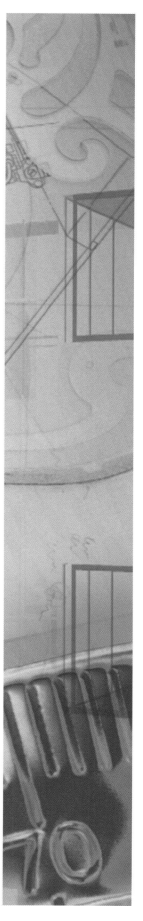

Love will:

a)   Move you to acts of kindness and mercy. Love is practical

b)   Move you to evangelise: most people become followers of Jesus and stay in church because of relationships. Who are you reaching? Who are you bringing?

c)   Move you to fellowship - even with people unlike you.

d)   Move you to your God-appointed destiny.

e)   Move you out in spiritual gifts: 1 Corinthians 14:12 points out that love motivates us to impart something for the benefit of others.

f)   Moves the church out of the building and into the city.

4.   Love That Builds Big

'from whom the whole body, joined and knit together by what every joint supplies, according to the effective working by which every part does its share, causes growth of the body for the edifying of itself in love.'
Ephesians 4:16

When God's love gets to work in our lives it overcomes smallness and small-mindedness. For this love knows that there are others to reach and others to help.

There are two things love provides in building the Church and changing our world:

a)   Contribution
b)   Connection

a)   Contribution

'Everyone has the opportunity to be great, because everyone has the opportunity to serve.'

i)   The Bible teaches us that we are each unique. (Psalm 139:14).

© Andrew Owen Reprinted 2015 email: dlr@destiny-church.com
Destiny Church, 70 Cathedral Street, Glasgow, G4 0RN
Follow us on Twitter @andrewdestiny @OwenSue @DLR3000   Visit our website www.destinyleadershipresources.com

ii)   You have gifts and talents that you must use. One day you will have to give an account for the way you have used them (Matthew 25:15).

iii)   Start small - stay faithful - become great.

> **'Yet it shall not be so among you; but whoever desires to become great among you, let him be your servant.'**
> Matthew 20:26

Jesus taught the way to greatness is traveled on the highway of service. There is to be no difference between 'laity' and 'clergy'. The Bible word for 'minister' nearly always means 'servant'.

iv)   It's not just serving that counts - but the way we serve! Ephesians 4:16 speaks of the 'proper' or 'effective' working of each part.

- With resolve and persistence
- With passion and energy
- With thought and imagination
- With attention and care
- With excellence and appreciation
- With submission and co-operation

b)   Connection

A healthy body functions by the proper connection between all the limbs, parts and organs. Likewise the Church body must connect, and you must get committed.

> **'not forsaking the assembling of ourselves together, as is the manner of some, but exhorting one another, and so much more as you see the Day approaching.'**
> Hebrews 10:25

The Church functions on three levels:

- The gathered community
- The intimate groups
- The ministry teams

These must serve with each other to build a highly effective Church, that is impacting its community.

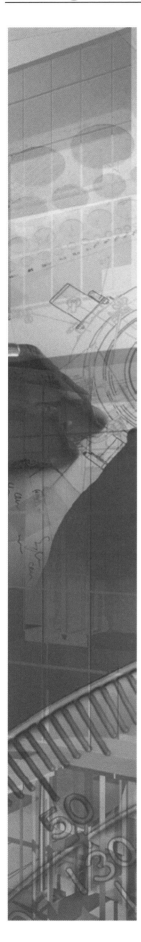

i) The Gathered Community

The early believers made a quality decision to start meeting on Resurrection Day - a Sunday - the first day of the week. They wanted to begin each week with God. Although we have no biblical argument to consider Sunday more holy than any other day, it is still a good time to meet. A gathered church meets to:

❖ Hear the word
❖ Pray for the nation (1 Timothy 2:2)
❖ Give and contribute (1 Corinthians 14:26)
❖ Praise and worship
❖ Reach the lost
❖ Be equipped to make a difference

We want these meetings to be:

❖ Relevant to our generation
❖ Passionate, strong and enthusiastic
❖ Ordered and effective
❖ Enjoyable and fruitful

ii) The Intimate Groups

As the church gets bigger, it is even more important to build meaningful relationships. Consequently small groups or fellowship meet regularly. It is important for you to be there. In these small groups we:

- Break bread as the Lord commands us

  'And they continued steadfastly in the apostles' doctrine and fellowship, in the breaking of bread, and in prayers.'
  Acts 2:42

- Learn to move in spiritual gifts
- Give to missions and reaching the world
- Pray for one another
- Welcome and look after new people
- Look at a lesson on truth and encouragement

These groups should be:

- Informal and friendly
- Non-threatening and non-religious
- Focused and purposeful

© Andrew Owen Reprinted 2015 email: dlr@destiny-church.com
Destiny Church, 70 Cathedral Street, Glasgow, G4 0RN
Follow us on Twitter @andrewdestiny @OwenSue @DLR3000   Visit our website www.destinyleadershipresources.com

iii) Ministry teams

Teams are created to make a difference. These ministry teams function both inside and outside the church. They are not only a great place to meet people and form real friendships, but a powerful potential way of impacting our world.

Don't Close The Circle

It is within human nature to close the circle. We all have a circle of friends, let's keep the circle open.

Jesus said:

> *'When you give a dinner or a supper, do not ask your friends, your brothers, your relatives, nor rich neighbors, lest they also invite you back, and you be repaid. But when you give a feast, invite the poor, the maimed, the lame, the blind. And you will be blessed, because they cannot repay you; for you shall be repaid at the resurrection of the just.'*
> Luke 14:12-14

We have an obligation therefore to include and invite as many as we can. Be a 'soul-bringer'.

Conclusion

James called the commandment we have been discussing a '<u>royal</u> command'.

> *'If you really fulfill the <u>royal</u> law according to the Scripture, "You shall love your neighbour as yourself," you do well;'*
> James 2:8

With our lives we want to give a 'royal command performance' - live a life that pleases God. To do this we must:

i)   Search our hearts: - Do I have my priorities right?
                            - Do I understand that the real issue is not 'how <u>much</u> I love', but '<u>who</u> I love'.

ii)   Am I involved?

iii) Is there fruit seen and developing in my life?

iv)   Is my life making a difference to anyone?

> *'Life is measured not by its duration, but by its donation.'*

This love overcomes all things. It brings heaven's resources to me and through me to others. This kind of love will stop the Church living inside four walls, and take it into the city and world beyond.

© Andrew Owen Reprinted 2015 email: dlr@destiny-church.com
Destiny Church, 70 Cathedral Street, Glasgow, G4 0RN
Follow us on Twitter @andrewdestiny @OwenSue @DLR3000   Visit our website www.destinyleadershipresources.com

My Personal Notes

Study 9

Leadership in the Advancing Church

My Personal Notes

© Andrew Owen Reprinted 2015 email: dlr@destiny-church.com
Destiny Church, 70 Cathedral Street, Glasgow, G4 0RN
Follow us on Twitter @andrewdestiny @OwenSue @DLR3000   Visit our website www.destinyleadershipresources.com

Leadership in the Advancing Church

We can see in the world two basic forms of government:

i)   Monarchy: Government by one person, called a king, general or dictator.

ii)   Democracy: Government by an opinion of the majority. Democracy comes from two words:

        demos = the people
        kratis   = to rule

We are very familiar with democracy. Leaders are appointed by the people for the people, and can be removed by the people.

However, the Bible introduces us to:

iii)   Theocracy: God rules.

        theo   = God
        kratis   = to rule

We read in Psalm 24:

> *'The earth is the Lord's, and all its fullness, the world and those who dwell therein.'*
> Psalm 24:1

When God wants something done-he appoints leaders to lead.

<u>Leadership</u> is God's way of doing things!

In the Old Testament we have examples like Moses (Exodus 3). In the New Testament we have examples like Paul (Acts 9).

Someone once said '*God so loved the world that He didn't send a committee!'*.

God appoints leadership in the church. This leadership is God's way of both caring for you and of accomplishing His mission.

Within His house He wants godly, courageous and caring leadership.

> *'Obey those who rule over you [your leaders], and be submissive, for they watch out for your souls, as those who must give account. Let them do so with joy and not with grief, for that would be unprofitable for you.'*
> Hebrews 13:17

In the Greek, the word 'leader' is 'hegeomai', and can mean ' to have the rule over you' ' to act as judge or governor'. Everyone needs to be accountable - who are you accountable to?

As we study the Bible, we can see that leadership in the Church is a team effort – but with clear headship. This is intended so that God's house does not end up being a haphazard pile of bricks, but a skillfully shaped building.

Peter describes us as 'living stones (1 Peter 2:5). For too long, many believers have lived in isolation or independence; they litter the country like bricks on a derelict site. Today, however, God has given particular gifts and then appointed certain offices to help the Church come through to its destiny. Where good leadership is in place and allowed to be strong, the Church prospers best.

The church's leadership team includes three categories of leaders:

❖   Sent leadership
❖   Securing leadership
❖   Support leadership

In this study we will look at the 'Sent' leadership. Securing and Support leaders are considered later.

Sent Leadership:

These are people directly sent and given by Christ himself! Sometimes they are called 'ascension gifts' or the 'five-fold ministries'.

> *'And He Himself gave some to be apostles, some prophets, some evangelists, and some pastors and teachers, for the equipping of the saints for the work of ministry, for the edifying of the body of Christ,'*
> Ephesians 4:11-12

They are listed as:

❖   Apostles
❖   Prophets
❖   Pastors
❖   Evangelists
❖   Teachers

They may be 'recognised' by men, but they are not 'appointed' by men. They are unique gifts and callings, chosen by God Himself. They are sent to accomplish a task. We need to have some understanding of how they work and function.

© Andrew Owen Reprinted 2015 email: dlr@destiny-church.com
Destiny Church, 70 Cathedral Street, Glasgow, G4 0RN
Follow us on Twitter @andrewdestiny @OwenSue @DLR3000   Visit our website www.destinyleadershipresources.com

a)   Christ - Centred

Jesus is the ultimate perfect leader. Someone once said:

'... of all the men that ever lived, of all the armies that ever marched, and of all the parliaments that ever sat. Considering all the kings that have ever reigned - no-one has affected the life of man upon the earth as much as this man Jesus.'

When Jesus was present on the earth, we can only find Him appointing Apostles, but when He arrived back in Heaven, He went to appoint a full ministry team that were truly representative of Him.

It is as if He has taken something of His own ability and placed it into others. They now carry His heart, plan, purpose and ability in these specific areas.

You might remember from your school days an experiment with light using prisms. It's a good illustration.

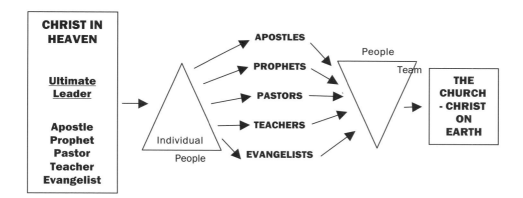

b)   Christ - Producing

Although Jesus lives physically in heaven, He is to be present on the earth through His Church.

'His intent was that now, through the church, the manifold wisdom of God should be made known to the rulers and authorities in the heavenly realms,'
Ephesians 3:10, NIV

Jesus has given Himself back to the church through these ministry gifts.

c)   Christ - Promoting

We have a very strong hope as believers.

i)   The Church will grow big and large, and affect the whole earth (Daniel 2:44).

ii)   That the gospel of Jesus Christ will be preached everywhere (Matthew 24:14).

iii)   That Jesus will one day return to a fully mature, fully ready Church. This day is compared to a marriage, where Jesus is the groom, and His Church a beautiful bride (Rev 21:2). These 'ascension gifts' are given to get us to this point!

They will: Get us serving effectively
             Help us grow maturely
             Help us live victoriously

Let's take a look at each of these ministries. They will promote a balanced church.

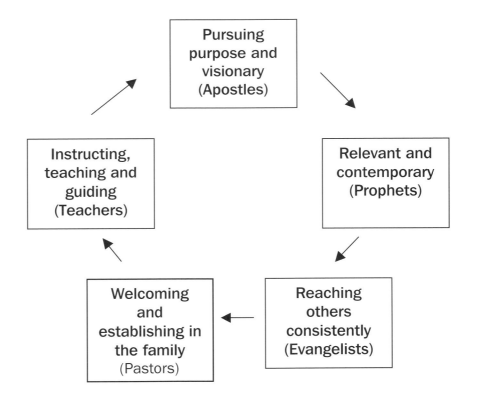

© Andrew Owen Reprinted 2015 email: dlr@destiny-church.com
Destiny Church, 70 Cathedral Street, Glasgow, G4 0RN
Follow us on Twitter @andrewdestiny @OwenSue @DLR3000   Visit our website www.destinyleadershipresources.com

Apostles

The calling of apostle was accredited to a number of men in the New Testament. We didn't find apostles in the old testament, Jesus introduced this ministry to build the church. There were the obvious twelve (Matthew 10:2), but also many others like Junias and Andronicus (Romans 16:7), and perhaps most notably – Paul (2 Corinthians 1:1).

> *'And God has appointed these in the church: first apostles ...'*
> 1 Corinthians 12:28

> *'According to the grace of God which was given to me, as a wise master builder I have laid the foundation,'*
> 1 Corinthians 3:10

We read 'first apostles'. They are first, not by their superiority, but by their necessity. They are sometimes the first into a new area to pioneer, and they become first in their ongoing leadership of the building programme.

Hallmarks Of Apostleship

i)   Calling (1 Corinthians 1:1; Galatians 1:1)

Apostleship is not a vocation chosen, neither is it an office aspired to, but a divine commissioning, called by God and recognised by men (Acts 9:6,10-18; Acts 13:2; Galatians 2:1-2).

ii)   Commission (Acts 26:16-18)

The term apostle literally means 'one sent forth'. He has been commissioned to accomplish a task, usually planting new churches or providing quality leadership in established churches.

iii)   Entrusted with truth (1 Corinthians 4:1; Acts 2:42).

iv)   Anointing and authority

Anointing is that sovereign seal of approval that produces success; it comes from God. Jesus claimed an anointing (Luke 4:18); any ministry must have it. Apostles have an 'apostolic anointing' which produces a depth of authority to see the job done.

'...according to the authority which the Lord has given me for edification ...'
2 Corinthians 13:10

This authority qualifies the apostle to make godly judgements, and it is this God-given authority that we should recognise and respect.

v)　Grace and perseverance

An envisioned man keeps his objective in sight. Not complacent with much activity, he will persevere where others give up, enduring frequent hardship and demonic hindrances. Grace will operate within him to continue with people where others quit, to see them come through to God's plan for their lives. (2 Corinthians 11:23-28). Rome wasn't built in a day; neither is God's house established in a moment. Most apostles face persecution of one kind or another as they are the forward advance of a movement. That's why we must pray for them.

vi)　Wisdom

'According to the grace of God which was given to me, as a wise master builder I have laid the foundation, and another builds on it. But let each one take heed how he builds on it.'
1 Corinthians 3:10

An apostle is not equipped to do all the tasks necessary for maturity, just as an architect is not skilled to wire, plumb or brick the house; but in effect he becomes the hub of the wheel, around him will orbit the other ministries, all playing their God-given part. His wisdom draws them in, in appropriate timing and order. His gift and calling give security and 'form' to the other ministries so that they function to maximum fulfilment.

vii)　Living letters

The 'proof of the pudding is in the eating' - if a man is an apostle you will see results like the churches Paul started.

'clearly you are an epistle of Christ, ministered by us, written not with ink but by the Spirit of the living God,'
2 Corinthians 3:3

© Andrew Owen Reprinted 2015 email: dlr@destiny-church.com
Destiny Church, 70 Cathedral Street, Glasgow, G4 0RN
Follow us on Twitter @andrewdestiny @OwenSue @DLR3000　Visit our website www.destinyleadershipresources.com

viii)   A man in relationship

While uniquely equipped, the human vulnerability of the apostle is safeguarded due to his willingness to work in harness and association with a company of men. (Galatians 2:1-2)

An apostolic community

The church must be an apostolic company. We would be foolish to believe that we can achieve our destiny without a proper connection to these kind of leaders. An apostolic company results in a <u>commissioned people, pursuing an unfolding vision, attaining to maturity as they go</u>.

Apostolic input will:

i)   Establish truth as a doctrinal basis of building (Acts 2:42). Every New Testament letter (Epistles) written to instruct, encourage or build the church was written by an apostle.

ii)   Help formulate strategy for pioneering advance. (2 Corinthians 1:16; 2 Corinthians 2:12; Acts 15)

iii)   Appoint other leaders for the godly oversight of the church through the laying on of hands. (Titus 1:5)

iv)   Draw in other ministries to add their dimension. (1 Thessalonians 3:2)

v)   Keep the local church looking out to a larger world. (1 Thessalonians 1:8)

vi)   Redistribute resources as need arises. (Acts 4:35)

vii)   Provoke the growth of new ministries. (Acts 16:1-3; (Acts 19:9-10)

viii)   Evangelise. (Acts 16:31)

ix)   Pray for and oversee the church through fatherly care. (Colossians 1:9; 3 John)

x)   Cause you to grow the church and advance the kingdom by helping you do <u>your job</u>!. (Acts 2:43-47; 5:12-16; 16:4-5)

xi)   Bring judgment, where necessary. (1 Corinthians 5:3)

xii)   Add some gift. (Romans 1:11)

Prophets

Although there were many prophets mentioned in the Old Testament, the New Testament prophets functioned in a different way.

'One who speaks forth or openly', would be one good definition of this term.

> *'having been built on the foundation of the apostles and prophets, Jesus Christ Himself being the chief cornerstone,'*
> Ephesians 2:20

Prophets are often inspirers and challengers, men enabled to perceive the mind of God for their times. They are caught up with the purposes of God and should help the church to be relevant, significant and effective.

Prophetic People

The church itself must be prophetic.

> *'A prophetic church is a people seeing a clear vision, motivated by a current word, experiencing an increasing burden.'*
> C J Mahoney

A prophetic community is not huddled away in some building, but involved with the world. They help the church fill its sphere of influence.

By being prophetic we do not just mean a people who are prophesying, but who are by their existence, lifestyle and message being a voice into the world, challenging society to live God's way, and embrace a different world order – kingdom order!

Earlier we learnt about God's concept of church – ekklesia – a powerful body changing the course of society. Jesus encourages us to be light and salt.

> *'You are the salt of the earth; but if the salt loses its flavor, how shall it be seasoned? It is then good for nothing but to be thrown out and trampled underfoot by men. You are the light of the world. A city that is set on a hill cannot be hidden.*
> Matthew 5:13-14

© Andrew Owen Reprinted 2015 email: dlr@destiny-church.com
Destiny Church, 70 Cathedral Street, Glasgow, G4 0RN
Follow us on Twitter @andrewdestiny @OwenSue @DLR3000   Visit our website www.destinyleadershipresources.com

Prophets will:

i)   Prophesy: move strongly in this gift and demonstrate a 'track record' of being able to hear God. (Acts 11:27)

ii)   Encourage the church. (Acts 15:32)

iii)   Sometimes bring direction. (Acts 11:27-30)

iv)   Participate in the commissioning of other ministries. (Acts 13:1-3

v)   Be always accountable to others (1 Corinthians 14:29)

vi)   Help people <u>know</u> God by a courageous life (Acts 15:27)

vii)   Help make the church socially relevant (Acts 11:27-30)

viii)   Keep the church on the cutting edge

> *'What is the prophetic ministry? – it relates to the full, original and ultimate purpose of God in and through his people.'*
> T Austin-Spark

Evangelists

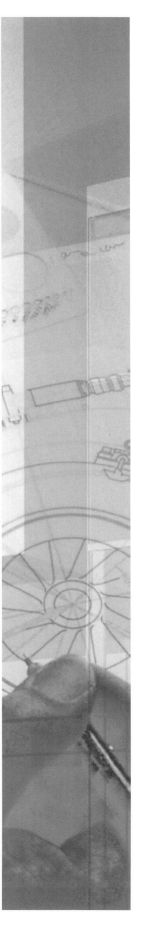

Some sources say that this term was used not originally for a ministry office, but rather by the military. The evangelist was a slave assigned to a general. During wars, battles and conflicts, women at home worried about their men. The evangelist was assigned with the task of running ahead of the general after the battle and declaring the news of his victory; likewise, the evangelist runs with news of victory won by Jesus.

Frequently, as was the case with Philip (Acts 8) he will run into virgin territory, breaking new ground, blasting out living stones at the quarry face. However, one must note that as with all Ephesians 4 ministries, they are first given to the Church for:

> *'... the equipping of the saints for the work of ministry,'*
> Ephesians 4:12

Evangelists will:

i)   Evangelise effectively. (Acts 8:5)

ii)   Provoke you to evangelise. (Ephesians 4:12)

iii)   Move in signs and wonders. (Mark 16:15-20)

iv)   Keep the Church reaching outwards. (Acts 8:40)

v)   Keep the proclamation of the message relevant. (Acts 8:30)

Pastors

Most of us are used to this title, but we don't always understand the concept. The word 'pastor' means 'shepherd'. We know that Jesus called Himself the 'Good Shepherd' (John 10:11). He 'shepherds' our lives by appointing 'under shepherds'.

A pastor or shepherd will:

i)   Lead you into a quality life through instructing you in God's Word. (Acts 20:27-28)

ii)   Raise up pastoral people to connect with you at good times and bad. (1 Timothy 3)

iii)   Keep spiritual food before you, so that even in pressure you will get through to success. (Mark 6:34)

iv)   Correct you when wrong. (1 Thessalonians 5:14)

v)   Protect the sheep. (John 10:11-13)

vi)   Have an undying love for the sheep. (Matthew 9:36-38)

vii)   Be on the alert for new sheep to be added. (John 10:16)

© Andrew Owen Reprinted 2015 email: dlr@destiny-church.com
Destiny Church, 70 Cathedral Street, Glasgow, G4 0RN
Follow us on Twitter @andrewdestiny @OwenSue @DLR3000   Visit our website www.destinyleadershipresources.com

Teachers

The title most often given to Jesus was 'teacher'. A teacher is given by God to the body to:

i)   Impart the apostolic doctrine (Acts 2:42; Titus 2:1)

ii)   Increase your knowledge of your inheritance (Hosea 4:6)

iii)   Challenge your mindset (Romans 12:2)

iv)   Make truth real, understandable and workable - prescribe as well as teach (1 Timothy 4:11)

v)   Inspire you to live at a higher level

vi)   Refute error (Titus 1:9)

vii)   Show you how to handle the Bible yourself (Colossians 3:16)

SUMMARY

A)   All Ephesians 4 ministries are there to:

1.   Get you fully functioning

2.   Help you to help others

3.   Bring the body to maturity

4.   Unlock the spiritual keys for growth, which include:

- unity (Psalm 133)
- every member functioning (Ephesians 4:16)
- ongoing momentum – 'they continued' (Acts 2:42) – keep on keeping on!
- proclaiming the gospel message (Romans 1:16)

B)   The Recognising of Ministries

Jesus said:

> **'You will know them by their fruits.'**
> Matthew 7:16

We are also aware by reading the Bible that there were many false prophets, apostles and teachers. Today there are also 'lone-ranger' prophets with strange messages, or people laying false claim to apostleship. Here are some guidelines:

1. Character counts. Jesus said by their fruits you would know them. You should look for:

    -   Integrity - their lives and words match up

    -   They are <u>not</u> covetous (2 Peter 2:1-3). False or suspect ministries often manipulate for financial gain.

2. The apostles were always recognised not only by the Church, but also within the company of other apostles.

3. Although the New Testament ministries were not afraid to use the names of 'apostle' or 'prophet', they did not pursue the title. 'Function matters more than Title.'

4. They were always working in some team setting and accountable in their life and teaching to others.

We become more effective by recognising and including God's resources for accomplishing our tasks.

What Should Our Response Be?

i)   If a gift from Christ - then gratefully receive.

ii)   If from Christ - He thinks them necessary - so should we.

iii) Honour and submit to their leadership.

iv)   Pray for them.

v)   Support in practical ways.

vi)   Prove loyal in friendship.

© Andrew Owen Reprinted 2015 email: dlr@destiny-church.com
Destiny Church, 70 Cathedral Street, Glasgow, G4 0RN
Follow us on Twitter @andrewdestiny @OwenSue @DLR3000   Visit our website www.destinyleadershipresources.com

Study 10

A Winning Team

© Andrew Owen Reprinted 2015 email: dlr@destiny-church.com
Destiny Church, 70 Cathedral Street, Glasgow, G4 0RN
Follow us on Twitter @andrewdestiny @OwenSue @DLR3000   Visit our website www.destinyleadershipresources.com

My Personal Notes

© Andrew Owen Reprinted 2015 email: dlr@destiny-church.com
Destiny Church, 70 Cathedral Street, Glasgow, G4 0RN
Follow us on Twitter @andrewdestiny @OwenSue @DLR3000   Visit our website www.destinyleadershipresources.com

A Winning Team

The Bible describes the Church as a body, a house or an army. Each of these functions when the independent units work as a team. The local church is to become a winning team - a team where each person finds their place and operates together.

> *'To complete each other is more important than competing with each other.'*

Jesus saw the Church as His winning team and said:

> *'... I will build my church and the gates of hell will not prevail against it.'*
> Matthew 16:18, KJV

To build this team we need:

- Vision
- Provision

A) Vision

> *'Where there is no vision, the people are unrestrained, But happy is he who keeps the law.'*
> Proverbs 29:18, NASB

Vision is for more than a set of goals. It's Hebrew word *'chazon'* literally means to 'see something' or to 'perceive a communication'.

According to the Bible, without vision your life will drift aimlessly, pointlessly and unproductively. A thriving church must have a clear vision, and the clearer it becomes, the more likely we are to achieve it.

God makes His vision clear, and expresses it in different ways.

> *' ... the earth will be full of the knowledge of the Lord As the waters cover the sea.'*
> Isaiah 11:9, NASB

or

> *'And this gospel of the kingdom shall be preached in the whole world for a witness to all the nations, and then the end shall come .'*
> Matthew 24:14

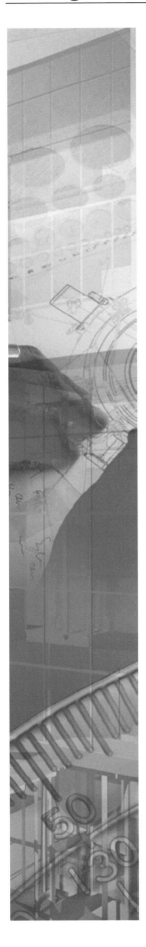

Then for you personally He says:

> *'For whom He foreknew, He also predestined to become conformed to the image of His Son, that He might be the first-born among many brethren;'*
> Romans 8:29

A church cannot have many visions because this becomes division. Yet inside the God-given vision, there will be room for everyone - as many projects and ministries are required to fulfil the vision!

We have already said that the Church is <u>His</u> Church. Each local church should be on a mission from heaven. We don't want good ideas, we want GOD ideas!

The vision will be:

◈ Given by God (Acts 26:19)

◈ Designated to an apostolic ministry (Acts 26:16)

◈ Established by the leadership team (Acts 20:27-28)

◈ Supported by the members (1 Corinthians 12:27)

◈ Effective in the world (Mark 16:20)

We have expressed our vision by the acronym **REACH.**
We want to:

Raise a championship church (Through Real Relationships)

Evangelise our region and nations beyond (Through effective testimony)

Accelerate Christian maturity (Through knowing truth & living it)

Champion the cause of Christ and His kingdom (Through a worshipful lifestyle)

Heal the hurting, and help the needy (Through using my gift in service)

Our vision is not only the accomplishment of a set of goals, but the values by which we operate to get to those goals, and the values that are found amongst us while they are yet being achieved.

© Andrew Owen Reprinted 2015 email: dlr@destiny-church.com
Destiny Church, 70 Cathedral Street, Glasgow, G4 0RN
Follow us on Twitter @andrewdestiny @OwenSue @DLR3000   Visit our website www.destinyleadershipresources.com

Vision = The pursuit of clear objectives whilst establishing a vibrant, godly, life-giving culture.

B) Provision for the vision

The vision cannot be realised unless there is provision made for it. It may be true to say 'where there is no vision the people perish', but it is also true to say that where there is no provision the vision remains unfulfilled.

This was the first reason given for the introduction of tithes and offerings:

> *'...that there may be food in my house...'*
> Malachi 3:10

God has made provision for you personally, and He has made provision for the Church, His house.

1. Personal provision

When God asked Adam to 'fill the earth and subdue it', He made provision for him so that the task was possible. He gave him a wife, and enough food to eat. (Read Genesis 1:26-31). This shows us God's benevolent nature. He has put several things in place for you which include:

i)   His Word - you should read it and know it
ii) Prayer - you should use it and grow it
iii) The Holy Spirit - you should know Him and walk with Him
iv) The Church - you should attend it and participate in it

If these factors are in place in our lives, we truly will have everything we need.

The Word	- introduces us to the promise of God, promises for provision, finance, protection, healing, forgiveness and much more
Prayer	- introduces us to the presence of God. God gets involved with our world
The Holy Spirit	- introduces us to the power of God, equipping us with supernatural gifts and fruitfulness
The Church	- introduces us to the family of God where we find mentors and leaders. We also find a family where we live life together.

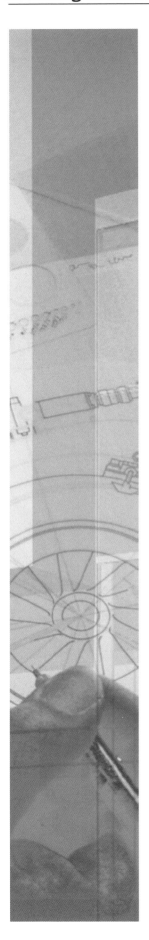

In many ways, God's family - the Church, is there to introduce us to a greater dimension of promises, presence and the power of God than we would find on our own. Through good mentoring and leadership we are taught how to live in the good of all God has made available. Part of this family includes leadership at another level - leaders we have called:

Securing Leadership

When 'Sent' leaders have been at work, people are gathered and results are seen. These people need to be secured in their faith, established in the vision, and encouraged into their destinies.

The Bible terms often used for these leaders were 'elders' or 'overseers' (1 Timothy 3:1).

Who Are The Securing Leaders?

Some of them may be 'sent ministries' as outlined earlier, combining their local involvement with a wider ministry. In the New Testament, Peter is an example of such a combination. He was an apostle but also an elder of the church in Jerusalem (1 Peter 5:1).

Sometimes these church leaders function voluntarily, while others could be released into full time ministry, supported by the local church.

> *'Let the elders who rule well be counted worthy of double honour, especially those who labour in the word and doctrine.'*
> 1 Timothy 5:17

In this verse the word 'honor' is literally 'honorarium' or salary.

Ideally each local church should have more than one such leader (James 5:14; Acts 14:23, 20:17; Philippians 1:1), although in the early stages it may have only one until others mature. Within the plurality of leaders, they will not operate as equals. Each one functions according to the ability and measure of grace and faith the Lord has given them.

> *'But to each one of us grace was given according to the measure of Christ's gift.'*
> Ephesians 4:7

We should note that these leaders are not a 'committee' that lead the church. But they are a team, being responsible together. We can see from scripture that often a local church is spearheaded by one person - God appoints a person, not a committee.

© Andrew Owen Reprinted 2015 email: dlr@destiny-church.com
Destiny Church, 70 Cathedral Street, Glasgow, G4 0RN
Follow us on Twitter @andrewdestiny @OwenSue @DLR3000   Visit our website www.destinyleadershipresources.com

For example: - James at Jerusalem (Acts 15:13)
 - The 'angel' (or minister) in Revelation 3
 - Even in the Old Testament we have
 examples like Moses or Joshua

The associate pastors assist the Senior Pastor in shepherding the church.

What Are Their Responsibilities?

1. Playing their part in the overall leadership team, using their skills and gifts when appropriate (Philippians 1:1).

2. Teaching the word of God (1 Timothy 3:2) according to:

    - The apostles' doctrine
    - The need of the moment

3. Maintaining the integrity of the church.
    Sadly the Church is mocked by the world due to its sin, compromise, and consequent feebleness. God's house was never meant to be like that. In fact the Bible states:

    > ***'For the time has come for judgment to begin at the house of God:'***
    > 1 Peter 4:17

    These leaders have a responsibility to maintain the integrity and unity of the house of God. In the event that they are unable to bring correction and repentance to a person through proper means (Matthew 5: Matthew 18), they are to remove a person from fellowship for one of the following reasons:

    i)   Immorality of any kind (1 Corinthians 5, 6;9)
    ii) Divisiveness (Titus 3:10)
    iii) Persistent, destructive behaviour. (1 Corinthians 5: 9-13)

    Although this course of action may be instigated by the elders and leadership team, it is enforced by the whole church.

4. Rebuke and correct on issues of the word (Titus 1:9)

5. Present every man mature in Christ (Colossians 1:28)

6. Disciple individuals and develop family life (1 Timothy 5)

7. Protecting
    i) From 'wolves' or heresy (Acts 20:29-30). 'Wolves' are people who try to infiltrate the Church for wrong motives. And either draw people away after themselves or cut them out from a good relationship with the Pastors and Church.

    ii) Sickness (James 5:13-15)

8.   Help and officiate at life-changing times
        - Baptisms
        - Baby dedication
        - Marriages
        - Death and funerals

9.   Be on hand for fatherly advice and godly counsel

Who Are These Securing Leaders to Be?

i)   Preferably Married Couples

> '*...appoint elders in every city as I commanded you - if a man is blameless, the husband of one wife ... For a bishop must be blameless,*'
> Titus 1:6-7

> '*This is a faithful saying: If a man desires the position of a bishop, <u>he</u> desires a good work.*'
> 1 Timothy 3:1

Since this role reflects the father in a family, the Bible appears to recommend <u>married</u> men, who can function from example and experience. Further, to function properly they need their wives at their side, so that they function as a team. In so many counselling situations a man could not function on his own, due to the need to maintain integrity and discretion, and the need for a woman's viewpoint and insight into a situation.

ii)   A Desire

> '*...If a man desires the position of a bishop, he desires a good work.*'
> 1 Timothy 3:1

While the ministries we spoke of earlier are callings, and gifts of the ascended Christ (Ephesians 4), this office is different in that it may be aspired to. A desire for maturity and responsibility is highly esteemed by the Lord.

iii) A Character Qualification!
The Bible highlights many character qualities that must be found in a man reaching for this position. Read 1 Timothy 3:1-9; Titus 1:5-9.

© Andrew Owen Reprinted 2015 email: dlr@destiny-church.com
Destiny Church, 70 Cathedral Street, Glasgow, G4 0RN
Follow us on Twitter @andrewdestiny @OwenSue @DLR3000   Visit our website www.destinyleadershipresources.com

The list includes:

a) Not suspect of a double standards life	i) Not a new Christian
b) Temperate	j) Just and fair
c) Sober	k) Able to teach
d) Good behaviour	l) Patient (grace evident)
e) Not addicted to drink	m) Holding fast the apostles' doctrine
f) Not greedy for money	n) Order and rule at home
g) Not covetous	o) One wife-including a good and healthy respect from their children
h) Not self-willed (ie themselves submissive)	

iv) Approved By God

While natural ambition can drive a man, ultimately only God will elevate the man.

> *'For exaltation comes neither from the east nor from the west nor from the south. But God is the Judge: He puts down one, And exalts another.'*
> Psalm 75: 6-7

v) Approved By Men

The scriptures teach us the important doctrine of the laying on of hands.

> *'Therefore, leaving the discussion of the elementary principles of Christ, let us go on to perfection, not laying again the foundation of repentance from dead works and of faith toward God, of the doctrine of baptisms, of laying on of hands, of resurrection of the dead, and of eternal judgment.'*
> Hebrews 6:1-2

The first line of leadership towards the church is apostolic, because these are 'sent' from God. Other leaders are not voted in, neither do they assume the role, but are appointed by the apostles to their tasks

> *'For this reason I left you in Crete, that you should set in order the things that are lacking, and appoint elders in every city as I commanded you'*
> Titus 1:5

© Andrew Owen Reprinted 2015 email: dlr@destiny-church.com
Destiny Church, 70 Cathedral Street, Glasgow, G4 0RN
Follow us on Twitter @andrewdestiny @OwenSue @DLR3000   Visit our website www.destinyleadershipresources.com   **115**

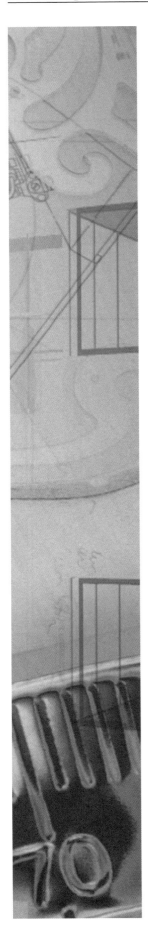

At the laying on of hands (usually called ordination):

- Authority is imparted
- Responsibility is imparted
- Accountability is imparted

When the correct people are appointed, the church is not surprised, and there is a wholesome accord by all.

vi) A Great Love for People

As this office is all to do with helping others, these securing leaders must have a love for people (1 Peter 5:2) and a very big passion for the church-the house of God.

© Andrew Owen Reprinted 2015 email: dlr@destiny-church.com
Destiny Church, 70 Cathedral Street, Glasgow, G4 0RN
Follow us on Twitter @andrewdestiny @OwenSue @DLR3000   Visit our website www.destinyleadershipresources.com

Study 11

Destiny

© Andrew Owen Reprinted 2015 email: dlr@destiny-church.com
Destiny Church, 70 Cathedral Street, Glasgow, G4 0RN
Follow us on Twitter @andrewdestiny @OwenSue @DLR3000   Visit our website www.destinyleadershipresources.com

My Personal Notes

Destiny

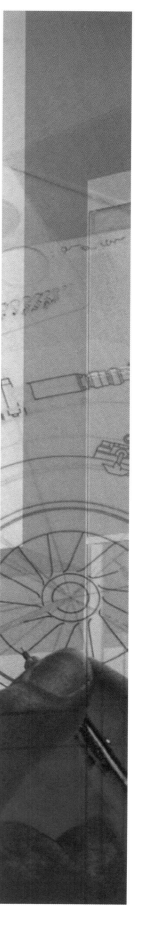

The dictionary defines destiny as:

> *'The purpose or end to which anything or anyone is appointed.'*

You are not a statistic or a number, but you were created by God to enjoy Him, and live for Him. To truly find your destiny you must:

Understand Eternal Life

What is eternal life? It is life, but not as we knew it! We read:

> *'For God so loved the world, that He gave His only begotten Son, that whoever believes in Him should not perish, but have eternal life.'*
> John 3:16, NASB

The Greek word for life is *'zoe', and means:*

> 'The state of one who is possessed of vitality'
> 'The absolute fullness of life'
> 'Life - real, genuine and vigorous, devoted to God'

While some think of eternal life as something that begins when you die, the Bible sees eternal life as something that begins when you give your life to Christ - and continues forever!

This kind of life should be evident in our lives and in the Church!

> *'for the kingdom of God is ...righteousness, peace and joy in the Holy Spirit.'*
> Romans 14:17

It is:

a) 'A joy-filled life'

> *'Though now you do not see Him, yet believing, you rejoice with joy inexpressible and full of glory.'*
> 1 Peter 1:8

Joy is a quality of life that is permanent - not an emotion that comes and goes with the circumstances of life.

Joy is based on a living active relationship with God – a confidence that He loves us, and is with us. This kind of happiness should be in you, and in our church meetings.

b) 'Hope-filled'

> *'This hope we have as an anchor of the soul, both sure and steadfast,'*
> Hebrews 6:19

Hope is defined as 'the happy anticipation of good'. Hope is the anchor of the soul. The believer expects the future to be bright because he has hope in God, this makes him an optimist.

c) 'Peace'

> *'and the peace of God, which surpasses all understanding, will guard your hearts and minds through Christ Jesus.*
> Philippians 4:7

When you have made your peace with God, there is peace available for you which the Bible describes as 'surpassing understanding'. You don't need to be stressed out or over-anxious. Let this peace settle in your hearts.

d) 'Faith activated'

> *'And this is the victory that has overcome the world – our faith.'*
> 1 John 5:4

Faith is an active response to any situation - It's making a choice. We chose to believe what God has to say about the situation.

© Andrew Owen Reprinted 2015 email: dlr@destiny-church.com
Destiny Church, 70 Cathedral Street, Glasgow, G4 0RN
Follow us on Twitter @andrewdestiny @OwenSue @DLR3000 Visit our website www.destinyleadershipresources.com

The Life of Faith

We live the life of faith by:

1.   Renewing our minds.

>   *'And do not be conformed to this world, but be transformed by the renewing of your mind, that you may prove what is that good and acceptable and perfect will of God.'*
>   Romans 12:2

Human beings are controlled through their thinking.

>   *'For as he thinks in his heart, so is he.'*
>   Proverbs 23:7

Align your thinking to that of God's truth.

2.   Learn that there is power in your tongue.

>   *'Death and life are in the power of the tongue, And those who love it will eat its fruit.'*
>   Proverbs 18:21

Don't speak negatively. Hold fast to a good confession.

3.   Develop your ability to praise and worship.

>   *'speaking to one another in psalms and hymns and spiritual songs, singing and making melody in your heart to the Lord.'*
>   Ephesians 5:19

Praise and worship are great keys to unlock your situation.

4.   Grow your prayer life.

At all times, and with different kinds of prayer.

>   *'Be anxious for nothing, but in everything by prayer and supplication, with thanksgiving, let your requests be made known to God;'*
>   Philippians 4:6

5. Grow your reading time

    Develop a daily devotional time. Read inspirationally - where God leads you, and read instructively - researching themes and subjects.

7. Meet with the church.

8. Listen intently to the preached word, take notes, and re-listen to a CD or MP3 downloads.

Reach for Your Destiny

You have a unique calling. Find it and enjoy it. Live for God in your home and workplace.

'For we are His workmanship, created in Christ Jesus for good works, which God prepared beforehand that we should walk in them.'
Ephesians 2:10

You will do this by realising:

© Andrew Owen Reprinted 2015 email: dlr@destiny-church.com
Destiny Church, 70 Cathedral Street, Glasgow, G4 0RN
Follow us on Twitter @andrewdestiny @OwenSue @DLR3000   Visit our website www.destinyleadershipresources.com

1. You Are Wanted

Regardless of the circumstances of your natural birth, you should know that God wanted <u>you</u>, and God created you.

> *'For you created my inmost being, you knit me together in my mother's womb. I praise you because I am fearfully and wonderfully made;'*
> Psalm 139: 13-14 NIV

In His sovereign ability as God, He thought of you, created you, and brought you into being for a purpose. He made <u>you</u> - and you are the only <u>you</u> He has!

2. You Are Needed

> *'For we are His workmanship, created in Christ Jesus for good works, which God prepared beforehand that we should walk in them.'*
> Ephesians 2:10

When God made you, He had a purpose in mind. Today people are trying to find purpose in such things as:

- Leisure
- Work
- Travel
- Knowledge

But you have a destiny - the purpose of God for your life. Find your purpose and you'll find your destiny. God has a bigger picture, it's like a jigsaw puzzle that He is assembling, you were made to fit into it. If you don't play your part the picture won't be complete, and you will not be fulfilled.

Question: From our earlier studies, what do you think the bigger picture is?

3. You Are Gifted

Jesus told a parable (Matthew 25:14-30) to illustrate a truth. Everyone has been given something that they must use. We learn from this story:

i)   The talent was given by another: God has given you something.

ii)   The gifts were for the benefit of the giver: You must use them to serve God.

iii)   They were called to account for their use; God will reward you for the way you have used them.

iv)   Not everyone had the same: we are all different.

v)   Each were responsible for <u>their</u> talents: Look at what you've got.

vi)   Those who did well were promoted with greater responsibility.

vii)   If we don't use the gifts we have got-then we will lose them.

A.   What Could These Gifts Be?

The Bible highlights many examples (Romans 12:6-8)

- Prophecy
- Ministry   (Serving)
- Teach/ Exhorts
- Substantial financial giving. Perhaps through business or enterprise
- Leadership
- Mercy

We are also given excellent examples in scripture of people like Dorcas (Acts 9:36) who made clothes and 'was always doing good'. She was so exceptional that when she died, she was the only person we read of who was so greatly missed that she just had to be raised from the dead!! Then there were people like Stephen (Acts 6:5) who became a project manager of a very significant task, and played a vital role in the advance of the early church.

> *'Everyone has the opportunity to be great - because everyone has the opportunity to serve.'*

Today there is incredible opportunity to make a difference, reach the lost and change our world. There has never been so much need, or so many ways to meet them and proclaim the wonderful gospel of Jesus Christ.

© Andrew Owen Reprinted 2015 email: dlr@destiny-church.com
Destiny Church, 70 Cathedral Street, Glasgow, G4 0RN
Follow us on Twitter @andrewdestiny @OwenSue @DLR3000   Visit our website www.destinyleadershipresources.com

Opportunities include:

Technicians:	TV/audio/MP3/IT/web
Artists/creative people:	Publishing/children/youth/media
Caring people:	Homeless/single parents/elderly
Administrative people:	Conference planning/schedules/office support
Musicians:	Live worship and praise/albums/ song writing/musicals
Teachers:	Children/new converts/prisons/ specialised issues eg marriage and family
Evangelists:	Streets/doors/drama/healing meetings/missions
Counsellors:	Debt/addictions
Builders & practical trades:	New buildings for church/ helping others
Missionaries:	New church plants/ orphanages/ compassion ministries
Drivers:	Buses and visitors
Pastoral People:	Asylum seekers/elderly/youth
Caterers:	Events/conferences/feeding programmes
Fund Raisers	Special projects/buildings

There is no end to the possibilities!

B.   How Do I Get Started?

Get started!!

a)   Identify your abilities as far as possible.

> *'that the sharing of your faith may become effective by the acknowledgment of every good thing which is in you in Christ Jesus.'*
> Philemon 6

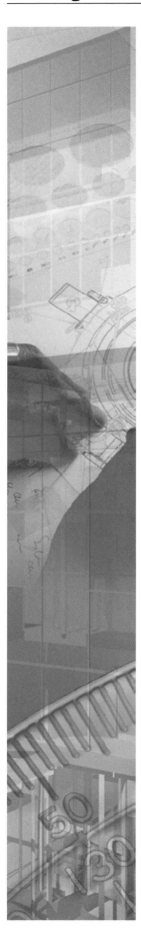

Passion <u>or</u> frustration is often an indicator of a gift. If you get frustrated because things are not organised well, you may be a good administrator. Passion and frustration can often be two sides of the same coin.

Ask yourself some questions

i)   Where have I seen fruit in my life?
ii)   What do others who know me say?
iii) How am I wired? Your personality usually suits your ability.

b)   Identify your opportunities

-    Is there a team already functioning in the church that you can join? Is it time to initiate a new venture?

-    What do you <u>see</u> that needs to be done and isn't being done? Do you need to discuss this with your leaders.

'Find a need and meet it,
find a hurt and heal it.'

© Andrew Owen Reprinted 2015 email: dlr@destiny-church.com
Destiny Church, 70 Cathedral Street, Glasgow, G4 0RN
Follow us on Twitter @andrewdestiny @OwenSue @DLR3000   Visit our website www.destinyleadershipresources.com

Study 12

Don't Stop Now!

My Personal Notes

© Andrew Owen Reprinted 2015 email: dlr@destiny-church.com
Destiny Church, 70 Cathedral Street, Glasgow, G4 0RN
Follow us on Twitter @andrewdestiny @OwenSue @DLR3000   Visit our website www.destinyleadershipresources.com

Don't Stop Now

A No-Limit Lifestyle

> *'When you limit yourself, you limit God. When you limit God, you limit yourself.*
> E L Cole

> *'Those who know their God shall be strong and do exploits.'*
> Daniel 11:32

> *'A man should believe for great things from God and attempt great things for God.'*
> William Carey

Having gone through this study, you should now reflect on 'where to from here?'

I want to encourage you that God can do, and does amazing things through imperfect people. I guess when He does, everyone knows it must have been God!

> *'But we have this treasure in earthen vessels, that the excellence of the power may be of God and not of us.'*
> 2 Corinthians 4:7

To live a 'no-limit lifestyle' you have to give yourself to it. Here are some things you should do now.

1. Start!

Meaningful Membership

Membership is biblical terminology!

> *For as the body is one and has many members, but all the members of that one body, being many, are one body, so also is Christ.'*
> 1 Corinthians 12:12

The word 'member' in Greek is 'melos', which literally means a 'limb of the body'.

A natural body cannot function properly without healthy limbs. Each believer should not only 'join' a church but become grafted into it - a functioning limb. Become a participating member.

When you become a member of the church, the leaders accept responsibility to lead you, and you in turn accept responsibility to play your part.

You can function on two levels:

i)   **Function by inputting positive attitudes**. These include things like encouragement, acts of mercy, giving, living right, and watching out for others.

ii)   **Function by accepting some responsibility.** This introduces us to the <u>third</u> level of leadership - **'support leadership'**.

SUPPORT LEADERSHIP

The Bible calls these support leaders 'helps ministries', 'administrations' or deacons. They are often department heads within a contemporary church.. (1 Corinthians 12:28)

The 'Helps' Ministry

The word 'help' literally means 'one who gives assistance'. They are like pillars in buildings, holding things up. They are to work alongside the other ministries and give assistance. The leadership team within the church is outworking a God-given vision. The support leadership team is there to help them get it done. One of the devil's most effective tactics is to keep the 'sent' leadership team so busy, they have no time to lead God's people properly, or to give themselves to the ministry of the word of God and prayer. The 'helps' ministry is to release them to do what they should be doing.

Examples are:

-    Numbers 11:17 - helpers given to Moses
-    2 Timothy 4:11-12 - Paul had helps ministries
-    Matthew 14:15-21 - 'helps' were required to administrate Jesus' miracles
-    Mark 14:12-16 - the 'last supper' preparations were handled by 'helps' ministries

How Should Support Leadership Function?

1.   Catch the spirit and 'culture' of the sent and securing leaders and developing church.

> *'Then I will come down and talk with you there. I will take of the Spirit that is upon you and will put the same upon them; and they shall bear the burden of the people with you, that you may not bear it yourself alone.'*
> Numbers 11:17

© Andrew Owen Reprinted 2015 email: dlr@destiny-church.com
Destiny Church, 70 Cathedral Street, Glasgow, G4 0RN
Follow us on Twitter @andrewdestiny @OwenSue @DLR3000   Visit our website www.destinyleadershipresources.com

When you become a part of a living church you become part of a different culture.

Catch the spirit of: Enterprise
                        Expectation
                        Excellence

2.   With faithfulness. Joshua served Moses for 40 years. The few references to him reveal him:

-    Washing Moses' hands and feet
-    Fighting the Amalekites while Moses prayed

Because of this 'schooling' he imbibed Moses' spirit and pressed forward with the people to take the land.

Faithfulness means consistency.
Faithfulness means loyalty.
Faithfulness means being focused and getting the job done.

> **'Like the cold of snow in time of harvest is a faithful messenger to those who send him, For he refreshes the soul of his masters.'**
> Proverbs 25:13

> **'Some will do their best, but leaders will do more - they will do what it takes!'**

3.   With vision. Having vision means 'to see something'. Support leaders should:

a)   Serve the apostolic vision, not have their own agendas (Exodus 17:11-12). God told Moses how to defeat the Amalekites - as Aaron and Hur entered into his vision and became his helpers, they then entered into his success.

b)   Train themselves in observation, so that they can themselves identify needs and fill them.

c)   Be supernaturally endowed with a spirit of excellence, grace and wisdom. This will, without doubt, produce a 'can do' mentality.

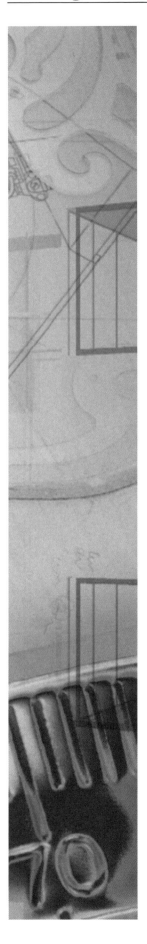

2. State!

State your intention! Most institutions have a mission statement these days. They may have spent considerable time getting their reason for existence down into one sentence. Make a quality decision on the direction of your life. What do you want to achieve, what has God called you to?

Many people spend more time planning their holidays than they do their lives! In the best way you know how, write down your goals for the next 1 year, 3 years and 10 years, then ask yourselves:

- Are the goals I have set achievable?
- Are the goals I have set going to lead me into my destiny?

> **'Where there is no vision, the people perish: but he that keepeth the law, happy is he.'**
> Proverbs 29:18 KJV

- Are these goals putting Jesus first in my life?

3. Step up!

Step up to another level. The call of God on our lives is always an 'upward call' - it takes us higher.

> **'I press toward the goal for the prize of the upward call of God in Christ Jesus.'**
> Philippians 3:14

To step up will mean a commitment to a lifestyle of change and challenge - but that's exactly what being a 'disciple' of Jesus Christ is all about! We <u>follow</u> him.

What is a Disciple?

True discipleship has three elements:

A disciple is a learner: Both the English and biblical words for 'disciple' come from the meaning 'to learn'.

A disciple is a follower: Jesus taught that a *'disciple ... will be like his teacher.' (Luke 6:40)*, that is, he not only learns from his teacher, but also walks in his footsteps – the goal being maturity and knowledge. Jesus' own disciples are good examples as people **'realized that they had been with Jesus.' (**Acts 4:13*)*

> **'If you abide in My word, you are My disciples indeed.'**
> John 8:31

A disciple is a doer: He does something!

© Andrew Owen Reprinted 2015 email: dlr@destiny-church.com
Destiny Church, 70 Cathedral Street, Glasgow, G4 0RN
Follow us on Twitter @andrewdestiny @OwenSue @DLR3000   Visit our website www.destinyleadershipresources.com

How Does Discipleship Take Place?

We are all to be disciples of Jesus, but as He is in Heaven can this happen? There are a variety of ways that God teaches and corrects; the primary way, however, is that discipleship takes place with good leadership.

> *'And you became followers of us*
> *and of the Lord,'*
> 1 Thessalonians 1:6

> *'Therefore I urge you, imitate me.'*
> 1 Corinthians 4:16

We learn from and follow the example of those who God has placed over us. Their instruction, correction and encouragement are God's means of shaping our lives to become more Christ-like. This involves far more than being a student of their teaching but must involve a following of their leadership.

> *'I urge you, brethren... that you also submit*
> *to such, and to everyone who works and*
> *labors with us.'*
> 1 Corinthians 16:15-16

Mentors: In a growing church family, you will always find good mentors – something few of us have had in life. Find someone further forward than you and build a mentoring relationship. Mentors will help you build your marriage, raise your kids, grow in your ministry or succeed in your business.

This takes place in a life context, not a classroom, so that:

❖ Your eagerness to learn must reach beyond meetings as you seek for your whole lifestyle to be shaped.

❖ There cannot be 'no go' areas - God sees no division between spiritual and secular. If you are submitted to Him, then this will be reflected in your response to His leaders.

❖ You must be prepared for leaders and others to address specific issues in your life, not only principles in general.

133

A Disciple's Attitudes

a) Teachability

Are you eager to learn new things? Are you open for others to show you how?

> *'The way of a fool is right in his own eyes,*
> *But he who heeds counsel is wise.'*
> Proverbs 12:15

b) Willingness To Change

Sometimes there is a sacrifice of personal ambitions or your own ways of doing things, in order to carry out tasks in the way and to the standard that someone else requires. It also means not hiding your weaknesses but opening your life up in a way that recognises the need to be strengthened – if you want a doctor to help you, you tell him your symptoms.

c) Servanthood

Discipling is on-the-job training. Your leaders will give you tasks to do that will build vital principles into your life and help you put into practice the things you have learned. This means we have to be servants, willing to do whatever it takes.

How To Receive Correction

Instruction and encouragement are not often difficult to receive, but correction can be another matter! A leader will be prepared to address issues and correct where necessary if he is to be faithful to you. How you handle this determines what fruit it bears in your life.

❖ **Don't Be Defensive:**

> *'Faithful are the wounds of a friend, But*
> *the kisses of an enemy are deceitful.'*
> Proverbs 27:6

❖ **Don't Make It A Personal Issue:** Receive correction as though from God himself (Thessalonians 2:13).

> *'And we urge you, brethren, to recognize*
> *those who labor among you, and are over*
> *you in the Lord and admonish you,'*
> 1 Thessalonians 5:12

© Andrew Owen Reprinted 2015 email: dlr@destiny-church.com
Destiny Church, 70 Cathedral Street, Glasgow, G4 0RN
Follow us on Twitter @andrewdestiny @OwenSue @DLR3000   Visit our website www.destinyleadershipresources.com

❖ **Don't walk away from unresolved conflicts**: Even if you find it difficult to accept the correction being brought, don't leave the matter without expressing your questions, hearing everything that is said and bringing the matter to a conclusion.

❖ **Don't read between the lines or look for hidden messages:** Listen carefully and look to understand fully the specific ways in which you are being asked to change.

❖ **Do Apply The Lesson To Be Learned:** Make sure you understand the action you need to take. Act on it as soon as possible and where appropriate ask for feedback as to how well you are succeeding.

Discipling the Nations

Discipleship is designed for rapid advance. If one evangelist brought 1,000 people to Jesus every day it would take over 13,000 years to reach the world. If every disciple were trained to win one person each year, it would only take 32 years.

> '*Many people shall come and say, "Come, and let us go up to the mountain of the Lord, To the house of the God of Jacob; He will teach us His ways, And we shall walk in His paths."*'
> Isaiah 2:3

All Called To Disciple

Every one of us will always be a disciple – hopefully always learning. In turn you should come to a place of discipling others – teaching them gently what you have learned.

Thankfully God always deals with us in a compassionate and grace-filled way, when it is our turn to disciple we should always treat others like that.

Here are some points:

❖ Don't forget where you have come from and the grace measured to you

❖ Don't try to remove 'splinters' from other people when you have a 'log' in your own life

❖ You are your brother's keeper, watch out for each other

❖ Never condemn or judge derogatively

◈ Don't attempt to control other people's lives. You can only encourage or counsel in line with what the Bible says.

◈ Disciple for excellence. God deserves the best!

We believe in the process of discipleship. All are called to grow and mature. Discipling in our lives is God's given way of personal growth.

4. Stay The Course!

Probably the two greatest attributes of a champion are endurance and perseverance. The two words sound the same but they mean different things.

Endure: To keep going when there are difficulties and challenges.

Persevere: To keep going on and up, reaching for the target and prize, it's keeping going with expectation..

> **'that you do not become sluggish, but imitate those who through faith and patience inherit the promises.'**
> Hebrews 6:12

God is not looking for those who were there at the beginning; He is looking for those who will be there at the end.

> **'Champions don't give up - they get up.'**

Conclusion

> **'That which we persist in doing becomes easier - not that the nature of the task has changed, but our ability and measure has.'**
> Emerson

The race of destiny is a life-long race! We must commit. People grow old 'young' these days. To grow old means you have stopped on the inside before God has stopped on the outside - keep going and enjoy the adventure.

© Andrew Owen Reprinted 2015 email: dlr@destiny-church.com
Destiny Church, 70 Cathedral Street, Glasgow, G4 0RN
Follow us on Twitter @andrewdestiny @OwenSue @DLR3000   Visit our website www.destinyleadershipresources.com

My Personal Notes

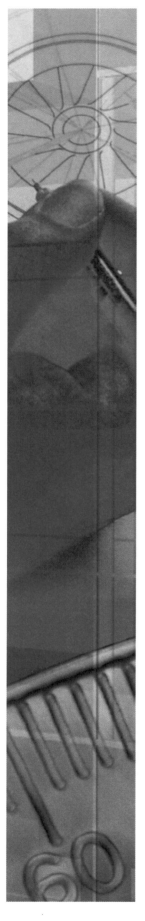

My Personal Notes

© Andrew Owen Reprinted 2015 email: dlr@destiny-church.com
Destiny Church, 70 Cathedral Street, Glasgow, G4 0RN
Follow us on Twitter @andrewdestiny @OwenSue @DLR3000   Visit our website www.destinyleadershipresources.com

My Personal Notes

My Personal Notes

© Andrew Owen Reprinted 2015 email: dlr@destiny-church.com
Destiny Church, 70 Cathedral Street, Glasgow, G4 0RN
Follow us on Twitter @andrewdestiny @OwenSue @DLR3000   Visit our website www.destinyleadershipresources.com

My Personal Notes

My Personal Notes

My Personal Notes

My Personal Notes